Born in 1925 in Martinique, Frantz Fanon studied medicine in France and later specialized in psychiatry. He was assigned to a hospital in Algeria during the war against the French. His experiences there led him to join the national liberation movement – for whom he became an important spokesperson. In this period, he wrote *The Wretched of the Earth*.

Fanon did not live to see Algeria liberated. In 1961, it was discovered that he was suffering from leukaemia; he died in December of that year. *Black Skin, White Masks* was first published in England in 1967.

BLACK SKIN, WHITE MASKS

FRANTZ FANON

Translated by

Charles Lam Markmann

First published in Great Britain 1986
PLUTO PRESS
345 Archway Road, London N6 5AA

Originally published in France as
Peau Noire, Masques Blanc

British Library Cataloguing in Publication Data
A catalogue record for this book is available from
the British Library

ISBN 0 7453 0035 9 pbk

09 08 07 06 05 04 03 02 01 00

15 14 13 12 11 10 9 8 7 6

Printed in the European Union
by WS Bookwell, Finland

CONTENTS

FOREWORD: REMEMBERING FANON
Self, Psyche and the Colonial Condition

O my body, make of me always a man who questions!
Black Skin, White Masks

In the popular memory of English socialism the mention of Frantz Fanon stirs a dim, deceiving echo. *Black Skin, White Masks*, *The Wretched of the Earth*, *Toward the African Revolution* – these memorable titles reverberate in the self-righteous rhetoric of 'resistance' whenever the English left gathers, in its narrow church or its Trotskyist camps, to deplore the immiseration of the colonized world. Repeatedly used as the idioms of simple moral outrage, Fanon's titles emptily echo a political spirit that is far from his own; they sound the troubled conscience of a socialist vision that extends, in the main, from an ethnocentric little Englandism to a large trade union internationalism. When that labourist line of vision is challenged by the 'autonomous' struggles of the politics of race and gender, or threatened by problems of human psychology or cultural representation, it can only make an empty gesture of solidarity. Whenever questions of race and sexuality make their own organizational and theoretical demands on the primacy of 'class', 'state' and 'party' the language of traditional socialism is quick to describe those urgent, 'other' questions as symptoms of petty-bourgeois deviation, signs of the bad faith of socialist intellectuals. The ritual respect accorded to the name of Fanon, the currency of his titles in the common language of liberation, are part of the ceremony of a polite, English refusal.

There has been no substantial work on Fanon in the history of the *New Left Review*; one piece in the *New Statesman*; one essay in *Marxism Today*; one article in *Socialist Register*; one short book by an English author. Of late, the memory of Fanon has been kept alive in the activist traditions of *Race and Class*, by A. Sivanandan's stirring indictments of state racism. Edward Said, himself a scholar engagé, has richly recalled the work of Fanon in his important T.S. Eliot memorial lectures, *Culture and Imperialism*. And finally, Stephan Feuchtwang's fine, far-reaching essay, 'Fanon's Politics of Culture' (*Economy and Society*) examines Fanon's concept of culture with its innovatory insights for a non-deterministic political organization of the psyche. Apart from these exceptions, in Britain today Fanon's ideas are effectively 'out of print'.

Memories of Fanon tend to the mythical. He is either revered as the prophetic spirit of Third World Liberation or reviled as an exterminating angel, the inspiration to violence in the Black Power movement. Despite his historic participation in the Algerian revolution and the influence of his ideas on the race politics of the 1960s and 1970s, Fanon's work will not be possessed by one political moment or movement, nor can it be easily placed in a seamless narrative of liberationist history. Fanon refuses to be so completely claimed by events or eventualities. It is the sustaining irony of his work that his severe commitment to the political task in hand, never restricted the restless, inquiring movement of his thought.

It is not for the finitude of philosophical thinking nor for the finality of a political direction that we turn to Fanon. Heir to the ingenuity and artistry of Toussaint and Senghor, as well as the iconoclasm of Nietzsche, Freud and Sartre,

Fanon is the purveyor of the transgressive and transitional truth. He may yearn for the total transformation of Man and Society, but he speaks most effectively from the uncertain interstices of historical change: from the area of ambivalence between race and sexuality; out of an unresolved contradiction between culture and class; from deep within the struggle of psychic representation and social reality.

To read Fanon is to experience the sense of division that prefigures – and fissures – the emergence of a truly radical thought that never dawns without casting an uncertain dark. His voice is most clearly heard in the subversive turn of a familiar term, in the silence of a sudden rupture: '*The Negro is not. Any more than the white man.*' The awkward division that breaks his line of thought keeps alive the dramatic and enigmatic sense of the process of change. That familiar alignment of colonial subjects – Black/White, Self/Other – is disturbed with one brief pause and the traditional grounds of racial identity are dispersed, whenever they are found to rest in the narcissistic myths of Negritude or White cultural supremacy. It is this palpable pressure of division and displacement that pushes Fanon's writing to the edge of things; the cutting edge that reveals no ultimate radiance but, in his words, 'exposes an utterly naked declivity where an authentic upheaval can be born'.

The psychiatric hospital at Blida-Joinville is one such place where, in the divided world of French Algeria, Fanon discovered the impossibility of his mission as a colonial psychiatrist:

> If psychiatry is the medical technique that aims to enable man no longer to be a stranger to his environment, I owe it to myself to affirm that the Arab, permanently an alien in his own country, lives in a state of absolute depersonalization . . . The social structure existing in Algeria was hostile to any attempt to put the individual back where he belonged.

The extremity of this colonial alienation of the person – this end of the 'idea' of the individual – produces a restless urgency in Fanon's search for a conceptual form appropriate to the social antagonism of the colonial relation. The body of his work splits between a Hegelian –Marxist dialectic, a phenomenological affirmation of Self and Other and the psychoanalytic ambivalence of the Unconscious, its turning from love to hate, mastery to servitude. In his desperate, doomed search for a dialectic of deliverance Fanon explores the edge of these modes for thought: his Hegelianism restores hope to history; his existentialist evocation of the 'I' restores the presence of the marginalized; and his psychoanalytic framework illuminates the 'madness' of racism, the pleasure of pain, the agonistic fantasy of political power.

As Fanon attempts such audacious, often impossible, transformations of truth and value, the jagged testimony of colonial dislocation, its displacement of time and person, its defilement of culture and territory, refuses the ambition of any 'total' theory of colonial opression. The Antillean *evolué* cut to the quick by the glancing look of a frightened, confused, White child; the stereotype of the native fixed at the shifting boundaries between barbarism and civility; the insatiable fear and desire for the Negro: 'Our women are at the mercy of Negroes . . . God knows how they make love';the deep cultural fear of the Black figured in the psychic trembling of Western sexuality – it is these signs and symptoms of the colonial condition that drive Fanon from one conceptual scheme to another, while the colonial relation takes shape in the gaps between them, articulated in the intrepid engagements of his style. As Fanon's text unfolds, the 'scientific' fact comes to be aggressed by the experience of the street; sociological observations are intercut with literary artefacts, and the poetry of liberation is brought up short against the leaden, deadening prose of the colonized world . . .

What is this distinctive *force* of Fanon's vision that has been forming even as I write about the division, the displacement, the cutting edge of his thought? It comes, I believe, from the tradition of the oppressed, as Walter Benjamin suggests; it is the language of a revolutionary awareness that 'the state of emergency in which we live is not the exception but the rule. We must attain to a concept of history that is in keeping with this insight.' And the state of emergency is also always a state of *emergence*. The struggle against colonial oppression changes not only the direction of Western history, but challenges its historicist 'idea' of time as a progressive, ordered whole. The analysis of colonial depersonalization alienates not only the Enlightenment idea of 'Man', but challenges the transparency of social reality, as a pre-given image of human knowledge. If the order of Western historicism is disturbed in the colonial state of emergency, even more deeply disturbed is the social and psychic representation of the human subject. For the very nature of humanity becomes estranged in the colonial condition and from that 'naked declivity' it emerges, not as an assertion of will nor as an evocation of freedom, but as an enigmatic questioning. With a question that echoes Freud's *what does woman want?*, Fanon turns to confront the colonized world. 'What does a man want?' he asks, in the introduction to *Black Skin, White Masks*, 'What does the black man want?'

To this loaded question where cultural alienation bears down on the ambivalence of psychic identification, Fanon responds with an agonizing performance of self-images:

> I had to meet the white man's eyes. An unfamiliar weight burdened me. In the white world the man of colour encounters

> difficulties in the development of his bodily schema . . . I was battered down by tom-toms, cannibalism, intellectual deficiency, fetishism, racial defects . . . I took myself far off from my own presence . . . What else could it be for me but an amputation, an excision, a haemorrhage that spattered my whole body with black blood?

From within the metaphor of vision complicit with a Western metaphysic of Man emerges the displacement of the colonial relation. The Black presence ruins the representative narrative of Western personhood: its past tethered to treacherous stereotypes of primitivism and degeneracy will not produce a history of civil progress, a space for the *Socius*; its present, dismembered and dislocated, will not contain the image of identity that is questioned in the dialectic of mind/body and resolved in the epistemology of 'appearance and reality'. The White man's eyes break up the Black man's body and in that act of epistemic violence its own frame of reference is transgressed, its field of vision disturbed.

'What does the black man *want*?' Fanon insists and in privileging the psychic dimension he changes not only what we understand by a *political* demand but transforms the very means by which we recognize and identify its *human agency.* Fanon is not principally posing the question of political oppression as the violation of a human 'essence', although he lapses into such a lament in his more existential moment. He is not raising the question of colonial man in the universalist terms of the liberal–humanist ('How does colonialism deny the Rights of Man?'); nor is he posing an ontological question about Man's being ('*Who* is the alienated colonial man?'). Fanon's question is not addressed to such a unified notion of history nor such a unitary concept of Man. It is one of the original and disturbing qualities of

Black Skin, White Masks that it rarely historicizes the colonial experience. There is no master narrative or realist perspective that provide a background of social and historical facts against which emerge the problems of the individual or collective psyche. Such a traditional sociological alignment of Self and Society or History and Psyche is rendered questionable in Fanon's identification of the colonial subject who is historicized as it comes to be heterogeneously inscribed in the texts of history, literature, science, myth. The colonial subject is always 'overdetermined from without', Fanon writes. It is through image and fantasy – those orders that figure transgressively on the borders of history and the unconscious – that Fanon most profoundly evokes the colonial condition

In articulating the problem of colonial cultural alienation in the psychoanalytic language of demand and desire, Fanon radically questions the formation of both individual and social authority as they come to be developed in the discourse of Social Sovereignity. The social virtues of historical rationality, cultural cohesion, the autonomy of individual consciousness assume an immediate, utopian identity with the subjects upon whom they confer a civil status. The civil state is the ultimate expression of the innate ethical and rational bent of the human mind; the social instinct is the progressive destiny of human nature, the necessary transition from Nature to Culture. The direct access from individual interests to social authority is objectified in the representative structure of a General Will – Law or Culture – where Psyche and Society mirror each other, transparently translating their difference, without loss, into a historical totality. Forms of social and psychic alienation and aggression – madness, self-hate, treason, violence – can never be acknowledged as determinate and constitutive conditions of civil authority, or as the ambivalent effects of the social instinct itself. They are always explained away as alien presences, occlusions of historical progress, the ultimate misrecognition of Man.

For Fanon such a myth of Man and Society is fundamentally undermined in the colonial situation where everyday life exhibits a 'constellation of delirium' that mediates the normal social relations of its subjects: 'The Negro enslaved by his inferiority, the white man enslaved by his superiority alike behave in accordance with a neurotic orientation.' Fanon's demand for a psychoanalytic explanation emerges from the perverse reflections of 'civil virtue' in the alienating acts of colonial governance: the visibility of cultural 'mummification' in the colonizer's avowed ambition to civilize or modernize the native which results in 'archaic inert institutions [that function] under the oppressor's supervision like a caricature of formerly fertile institutions'; or the validity of violence in the very definition of the colonial social space; or the viability of the febrile, fantasmatic images of racial hatred that come to be absorbed and acted out in the wisdom of the West. These interpositions, indeed collaborations of political and psychic violence *within* civic virtue, alienation within identity, drive Fanon to describe the splitting of the colonial space of consciousness and society as marked by a 'Manichean delirium'.

The representative figure of such a perversion, I want to suggest, is the image of post-Enlightenment man tethered to, *not* confronted by, his dark reflection, the shadow of colonized man, that splits his presence, distorts his outline, breaches his boundaries, repeats his action at a distance, disturbs and divides the very time of his being. This ambivalent identification of the racist world – moving on two planes without being in the least embarrassed by it, as Sartre says of the anti-Semitic consciousness – turns on the idea of Man *as* his alienated image, not Self and Other but the 'Otherness' of the Self inscribed in the perverse palimpsest of colonial identity. And it is that bizarre figure of desire, which splits along the axis on which it turns, that compels Fanon to put the psychoanalytic question of the desire of the subject to the historic condition of colonial man.

'What is often called the black soul is a white man's artefact,' Fanon writes. This transference, I've argued, speaks otherwise. It reveals the deep psychic uncertainty of the colonial relation itself; its split representations stage that division of 'body' and 'soul' which enacts the artifice of 'identity'; a division which cuts across the fragile skin – black and white – of individual and social authority. What emerges from the figurative language I have used to make such an argument, are three conditions that underlie an understanding of the *process of identification* in the analytic of desire.

First: to exist is to be called into being in relation to an Otherness, its look or locus. It is a demand that reaches outward to an external object and as J. Rose writes, 'it is the relation of this demand to the place of the object it claims that becomes the basis for identification'. This process is visible in that exchange of looks between native and settler that structures their psychic relation in the paranoid fantasy of boundless possession and its familiar language of reversal: 'when their glances meet he [the settler] ascertains bitterly, always on the defensive, "They want to take our place." It is true for there is no native who does not dream at least once a day of setting himself up in the settler's place.' It is always in relation to the place of the Other that colonial desire is articulated: that is, in part, the fantasmatic space of 'possession' that no one subject can singly occupy which permits the dream of the inversion of roles.

Second: the very place of identification, caught in the tension of demand and desire, is a space of splitting. The fantasy of the native is precisely to occupy the master's place while keeping his place in the slave's *avenging* anger. 'Black skins, white masks' is not, for example, a neat division; it is a doubling, dissembling image of being in at least two places at once which makes it impossible for the devalued, insatiable evolué (an abandonment neurotic, Fanon claims) to accept the colonizer's invitation to identity: 'You're a doctor, a writer, a student, you're *different* you're one of *us*.' It is precisely in that ambivalent use of 'different' – to be different from those that are different makes you the same – that the Unconscious speaks of the form of Otherness, the tethered shadow of deferral and displacement. It is not the Colonialist Self or the Colonized Other, but the disturbing distance in–between that constitutes the figure of colonial otherness – the White man's artifice inscribed on the black man's body. It is in relation to this impossible object that emerges the liminal problem of colonial identity and its vicissitudes.

Finally, as has already been disclosed by the rhetorical figures of my account of desire and Otherness, the question of identification is never the affirmation of a pre-given identity, never a self-fulfilling prophecy – it is always the production of an 'image' of identity and the transformation of the subject in assuming that image. The demand of identification – that is, to be *for* an Other – entails the representation of the subject in the differentiating order of Otherness. Identification, as we inferred from the illustrations above, is always the return of an image of identity which bears the mark of splitting in that 'Other' place from which it comes. For Fanon, like Lacan, the primary moments of such a repetition of the self lie in the desire of the look and the limits of language. The 'atmosphere of certain uncertainty' that surrounds the body certifies its existence and threatens its dismemberment.

> Look a Negro . . . Mama, see the Negro! I'm frightened . . . I could no longer laugh, because I already know there were legends, stories, history and above all *historicity* . . . Then assailed at various points, the corporal schema crumbled its place taken by a racial epidermal schema . . . It was no longer a question of being aware of my body in the third person but in a triple person . . . I was responsible for my body, for my race, for my ancestors.

In reading *Black Skin, White Masks* it is crucial to respect the difference between 'personal identity' as an intimation of reality, or an intuition of being, and the psychoanalytic problem of identification that, in a sense, always begs the question of the subject – 'What does a man want?' The emergence of the human subject as socially and psychically authenticated depends upon the *negation* of an originary narrative of fulfilment or an imaginary coincidence between individual interest or instinct and the General Will. Such binary, two-part, identities function in a kind of narcissistic reflection of the One in the Other which is confronted in the language of desire by the psychoanalytic process of identification. For identification, identity is never an *a priori*, nor a finished product; it is only ever the problematic process of access to an 'image' of totality. The discursive conditions of this psychic image of identification will be clarified if we think of the perilous perspective of the concept of the image itself. For the image – as point of identification – marks the site of an ambivalence. Its representation is always spatially split – it makes *present* something that is *absent* – and temporally deferred – it is the representation of a time that is always elsewhere, a repetition. The image is only ever an *appurtenance* to authority and identity; it must never be read mimetically as the 'appearance' of a 'reality'. The access to the image of identity is only ever possible in the *negation* of any sense of originality or plenitude, through the principle of displacement and differentiation (absence/presence; representation/repetition) that always renders it a liminal reality. The image is at once a metaphoric substitution, an illusion of presence and by that same token a metonym, a sign of its absence and loss. It is precisely from this edge of meaning and being, from this shifting boundary of otherness within identity, that Fanon asks: 'What does a *black* man want?'

> When it encounters resistance from the other, self-consciousness undergoes the experience of desire . . . As soon as I desire I ask to be considered. I am not merely here and now, sealed into thingness. I am for somewhere else and for something else. I demand that notice be taken of my negating activity in so far as I pursue something other than life . . .
>
> I occupied space. I moved towards the other . . . and the evanescent other, hostile but not opaque, transparent, not there, disappeared. Nausea.

From that overwhelming emptiness of nausea Fanon makes his answer: the black man wants the objectifying confrontation with otherness; in the colonial psyche there is an unconscious disavowal of the negating, splitting moment of desire. The place of the Other must not be imaged as Fanon sometimes suggests as a fixed phenomenological point, opposed to the self, that represents a culturally alien consciousness. The Other must be seen as the necessary negation of a primordial identity – cultural or psychic – that introduces the system of differentiation which enables the 'cultural' to be signified as a linguistic, symbolic, historic reality. If, as I have suggested, the subject of desire is never simply a Myself, then the Other is never simply an *It-self*, a font of identity, truth, or misrecognition.

As a principle of identification, the Other bestows a degree of objectivity but its representation – be it the social process of the Law or the psychic process of the Oedipus – is always ambivalent, disclosing a lack. For instance, the common, conversational distinction between 'the letter and spirit' of the Law displays the otherness of Law itself; the ambiguous grey area between 'Justice' and judicial procedure is, quite literally, a conflict of judgement. In the language of psychoanalysis, the Law of the Father or the paternal metaphor, again, cannot be taken at its word. It is a process of substitution and exchange that inscribes a normative, normalizing place for the subject; but that metaphoric access to identity is exactly the place of prohibition and repression, precisely a conflict of authority. Identification, as it is spoken in the *desire of the Other*, is always a question of interpretation for it is the elusive assignation of myself with a one-self, the elision of person and place.

If the differentiating force of the Other is the process of the subject's signification in language and society's objectification in Law, then how can the Other disappear? Can desire, the moving spirit of the subject ever, evanesce?

In his more analytic mode Fanon can impede the exploration of these ambivalent, uncertain questions of colonial desire. The state of emergency from which he writes demands more insurgent answers, more immediate identifications. At times Fanon attempts too close a correspondence between the *mise-en-scène* of unconscious fantasy and the phantoms of racist fear and hate that stalk the colonial scene; he turns too hastily from the ambivalences of identification to the antagonistic identities of political alienation and cultural discrimination; he is too quick to name the Other, to personalize its presence in the language of colonial racism – 'the real Other for the white man is and will continue to be the black man. And conversely.' These attempts, in Fanon's words, to restore the dream to its proper political time and cultural space can, at times, blunt the edge of Fanon's brilliant illustrations of the complexity of psychic projections in the pathological colonial relation. Jean Veneuse, the Antillean evolué, desires not merely to be in the place of the White man but compulsively seeks to look back and down on himself from that position. The White man does not merely deny what he fears and desires by projecting it on 'them'; Fanon sometimes forgets that paranoia never preserves its position of power for the compulsive identification with a persecutory 'They' is always an evacuation and emptying of the 'I'.

Fanon's sociodiagnostic psychiatry tends to explain away the ambivalent turns and returns of the subject of colonial desire, its masquerade of Western Man and the 'long' historical perspective. It is as if Fanon is fearful of his most radical insights: that the space of the body and its identification is a representational reality; that the politics of race will not be entirely contained within the humanist myth of man or economic necessity or historical progress, for its psychic affects questions such forms of determinism; that social sovereignity and human subjectivity are only realizable in the order of Otherness. It is as if the question of desire that emerged from the traumatic tradition of the oppressed has to be denied, at the end of *Black Skin, White Masks*, to make way for an existentialist humanism that is as banal as it is beatific:

> Why not the quite simple attempt to touch the other to feel the other, to explain the other to myself? . . . At the conclusion of this study, I want the world to recognize, with me, the open door of every consciousness.

Such a deep hunger for humanism, despite Fanon's insight into the dark side of Man, must be an overcompensation for the closed consciousness or 'dual narcissism' to which he attributes the depersonalization of colonial man: 'There one lies body to body, with one's blackness or one's whiteness in full narcissistic cry, each sealed into his own particularity – with, it is true, now and then a flash or so.' It is this flash of 'recognition' – in its Hegelian sense with its transcendental, sublative spirit – that fails to ignite in the colonial relation where there is only narcissistic indifference: 'And yet the Negro knows there is a difference. He wants it . . . The former slave needs a challenge to his humanity'. In the absence of such a challenge, Fanon argues, the colonized can only imitate, never identify, a distinction nicely made by the psychoanalyst Annie Reich: 'It is imitation . . . when the child holds the newspaper *like* his father. It is identification when the child learns to read.' In disavowing the culturally differentiated condition of the colonial world – in demanding '*Turn White or disappear*' – the colonizer is himself caught in the ambivalence of paranoic identification, alternating between fantasies of megalomania and persecution.

However Fanon's Hegelian dream for a human reality *in-itself-for itself* is ironized, even mocked, by his view of the Manichean structure of colonial consciousness and its non-dialectical division. What he says in *The Wretched of the Earth* of the demography of the colonial city reflects his view of the psychic structure of the colonial relation. The native and settler zones, like the juxtaposition of black and white bodies, are opposed, but not in the service of 'a higher unity'. No concilation is possible, he concludes, for of the two terms onc is superfluous.

No, there can be no reconciliation, no Hegelian 'recognition', no simple, sentimental promise of a humanistic 'world of the You.' Can there be life without transcendence? Politics without the dream of perfectibility? Unlike Fanon, I think the *non-dialectical* moment of Manicheanism suggests an answer. By following the trajectory of colonial desire – in the company of that bizarre colonial figure, the tethered shadow – it becomes possible to cross, even to shift the Manichean boundaries. Where there is no human *nature* hope can hardly spring eternal; but it emerges surely and surreptitiously in the strategic return of that difference that informs and deforms the image of identity, in the margin of Otherness that displays identification. There may be no Hegelian negation but Fanon must sometimes be reminded that the disavowal of the Other always exacerbates the 'edge' of identification, reveals that dangerous place where identity and aggressivity are twinned. For denial is always a retroactive process; a *half* acknowledgement of that Otherness which has left its traumatic mark. In that uncertainty lurks the white masked black man; and from such ambivalent identification – black skin, white masks – it is possible, I believe, to redeem the pathos of cultural confusion into a strategy of political subversion. We cannot agree with Fanon that 'since the racial drama is played out in the open the black man has no time to make it unconscious', but that is a provocative thought. In occupying two places at once – or three in Fanon's case – the depersonalized, dislocated colonial subject can become an incalculable object, quite literally, difficult to place. The demand of authority cannot unify its message nor simply identify its subjects. For the strategy of colonial desire is to stage the drama of identity at the point at which the black mask *slips* to reveal the white skin. At that edge, in between the black body and the white body, there is a tension of meaning and being, or some would say demand and desire, which is the psychic counterpart to that 'muscular tension' that inhabits the native body:

> The symbols of social order – the police, the bugle calls in the barracks, military parades and the waving flags – are at one and

> the same time inhibitory and stimulating: for they do not convey the message 'Don't dare to budge'; rather, they cry out 'Get ready to attack'.

It is from that tension – both psychic and political – that a strategy of subversion emerges. It is a mode of negation that seeks not to unveil the fullness of Man but to manipulate his representation. It is a form of power that is exercised at the very limits of identity and authority, in the mocking spirit of mask and image; it is the lesson taught by the veiled Algerian woman in the course of the Revolution as she crossed the Manichean lines to claim her liberty. In Fanon's essay *Algeria Unveiled* the colonizer's attempt to unveil the Algerian woman does not simply turn the veil into a symbol of resistance; it becomes a technique of camouflage, a means of struggle – the veil conceals bombs. The veil that once secured the boundary of the home – the limits of woman – now masks the woman in her revolutionary activity, linking the Arab city and the French quarter, transgressing the familial and colonial boundary. As the 'veil' is liberated in the public sphere, circulating between and beyond cultural and social norms and spaces, it becomes the object of paranoid surveillance and interrogation. Every veiled woman, writes Fanon, became suspect. And when the veil is shed in order to penetrate deeper into the European quarter, the colonial police see everything and nothing. An Algerian woman is only, after all, a woman. But the Algerian *fidai* is an arsenal and in her handbag she carries her hand-grenades.

Remembering Fanon is a process of intense discovery and disorientation. Remembering is never a quiet act of introspection or retrospection. It is a painful re-membering, a putting together of the dismembered past to make sense of the trauma of the present. It is such a memory of the history of race and racism, colonialism and the question of cultural identity, that Fanon reveals with greater profundity and poetry than any other writer. What he achieves, I believe, is something far greater: for in seeing the phobic image of the Negro, the native, the colonized, deeply woven into the psychic pattern of the West, he offers the master and slave a deeper reflection of their interpositions, as well as the hope of a difficult, even dangerous, freedom: 'It is through the effort to recapture the self and to scrutinize the self, it is through the lasting tension of their freedom that men will be able to create the ideal conditions of existence for a human world.' Nobody writes with more honesty and insight of this lasting tension of freedom in which the self – the peremptory self of the present – disavows an image of itself as an orginary past or an ideal future and confronts the paradox of its own making.

For Fanon, in *Black Skin, White Masks*, there is the intricate irony of turning the European existentialist and psychoanalytic traditions to face the history of the Negro which they had never contemplated, to face the reality of Fanon himself. This leads to a meditation on the experience of dispossession and dislocation – psychic and social – which speaks to the condition of the marginalized, the alienated, those who have to live under the surveillance of a sign of identity and fantasy that denies their difference. In shifting the focus of cultural racism from the politics of nationalism to the politics of narcissism, Fanon opens up a margin of interrogation that, causes a subversive slippage of identity and authority. Nowhere is this slippage more visible than in his work itself where a range of texts and traditions – from the classical repertoire to the quotidien, conversational culture of racism – vie to utter that last word which remains unspoken. Nowhere is this slippage more significantly experienced than in the impossibility of inferring from the texts of Fanon a pacific image of 'society' or the 'state' as a homogeneous philosophical or representational unity. The 'social' is always an unresolved ensemble of antagonistic interlocutions between positions of power and poverty, knowledge and oppression, history and fantasy, surveillance and subversion. It is for this reason – above all else – in the twenty-fifth anniversary of his death, that we should turn to Fanon.

In Britain, today, as a range of culturally and racially marginalized groups readily assume the mask of the Black not to deny their diversity but to audaciously announce the important artifice of cultural identity and its difference, the need for Fanon becomes urgent. As political groups from different directions gather under the banner of the Black, not to homogenize their oppression but to make of it a common cause, a public image of the identity of otherness, the need for Fanon becomes urgent. Urgent, in order to remind us of that crucial engagement between mask and identity, image and identification, from which comes the lasting tension of our freedom and the lasting impression of ourselves as others.

> In the case of display . . . the play of combat in the form of intimidation, the being gives of himself, or receives from the other, something that is like a mask, a double, an envelope, a thrown-off skin, thrown off in order to cover the frame of a shield. It is through this separated form of himself that the being comes into play in his effects of life and death. [Jacques Lacan]

The time has come to return to Fanon; as always, I believe, with a question: How can the human world live its difference? how can a human being live Other-wise?

Homi K. Bhabha
London 1986

NOTE

Fanon's use of the word 'man' usually connotes a phenomenological quality of humanness, inclusive of man and woman and, for that very reason, ignores the question of gender difference. The problem stems from Fanon's desire to site the question of sexual difference within the problematic of cultural difference – to give them a shared origin – which is suggestive, but often simplifies the question of sexuality. His portrayals of white women often collude with their cultural stereotypes and reduce the 'desire' of sexuality to the desire for sex, leaving unexplored the elusive function of the 'object' of desire. In chapter 6 he attempts a somewhat more complex reading of masochism but in making the Negro the '*predestined* depository of this aggression' [my emphasis] he again pre-empts a fuller psychoanalytic discussion of the production of psychic aggressivity in identification and its relation to cultural difference, by citing the cultural stereotype as the predestined aim of the sexual drive. Of the woman of colour he has very little to say. 'I know nothing about her,' he writes in *Black Skin, White Masks*. This crucial issue requires an order of psychoanalytic argument that goes well beyond the scope of my foreword. I have therefore chosen to note the importance of the problem rather than to elide it in a facile charge of 'sexism'.

ACKNOWLEDGEMENTS

Thanks to Stephan Feuchtwang for shepherding these ideas; Stuart Hall for discussing them; A. Sivanandan and Hazel Walters for their archival assistance at the Institute of Race Relations; Pete Ayrton for his patience; and Jackie Bhabha for the engaged combat of comrades.

Translator's Note

I would like to acknowledge the contributions made to this translation by André Leveillé of Rome, Italy, and Doctors Ruth M. and William F. Murphy of Lincoln and Boston, Massachusetts. To M. Leveillé I am indebted for many clarifications of French terms and slang, on certain events of the postwar period that received more attention in France than in America, on relevant details of daily life in France, and on matters Antillean and Algerian. To the Doctors Murphy I am grateful for help with the terminology of psychology and psychiatry and elucidations on European practices in the field.

—C.L.M.

INTRODUCTION

> *I am talking of millions of men who have been skillfully injected with fear, inferiority complexes, trepidation, servility, despair, abasement.*
>
> —*Aimé Césaire,* Discours sur le Colonialisme

The explosion will not happen today. It is too soon . . . or too late.

I do not come with timeless truths.

My consciousness is not illuminated with ultimate radiances.

Nevertheless, in complete composure, I think it would be good if certain things were said.

These things I am going to say, not shout. For it is a long time since shouting has gone out of my life.

So very long. . . .

Why write this book? No one has asked me for it.

Especially those to whom it is directed.

Well? Well, I reply quite calmly that there are too many idiots in this world. And having said it, I have the burden of proving it.

Toward a new humanism. . . .

Understanding among men. . . .

Our colored brothers. . . .

Mankind, I believe in you. . . .

Race prejudice. . . .

To understand and to love. . . .

From all sides dozens and hundreds of pages assail

me and try to impose their wills on me. But a single line would be enough. Supply a single answer and the color problem would be stripped of all its importance.

What does a man want?

What does the black man want?

At the risk of arousing the resentment of my colored brothers, I will say that the black is not a man.

There is a zone of nonbeing, an extraordinarily sterile and arid region, an utterly naked declivity where an authentic upheaval can be born. In most cases, the black man lacks the advantage of being able to accomplish this descent into a real hell.

Man is not merely a possibility of recapture or of negation. If it is true that consciousness is a process of transcendence, we have to see too that this transcendence is haunted by the problems of love and understanding. Man is a *yes* that vibrates to cosmic harmonies. Uprooted, pursued, baffled, doomed to watch the dissolution of the truths that he has worked out for himself one after another, he has to give up projecting onto the world an antinomy that coexists with him.

The black is a black man; that is, as the result of a series of aberrations of affect, he is rooted at the core of a universe from which he must be extricated.

The problem is important. I propose nothing short of the liberation of the man of color from himself. We shall go very slowly, for there are two camps: the white and the black.

Stubbornly we shall investigate both metaphysics and we shall find that they are often quite fluid.

We shall have no mercy for the former governors, the former missionaries. To us, the man who adores the Negro is as "sick" as the man who abominates him.

Conversely, the black man who wants to turn his race

white is as miserable as he who preaches hatred for the whites.

In the absolute, the black is no more to be loved than the Czech, and truly what is to be done is to set man free.

This book should have been written three years ago. . . . But these truths were a fire in me then. Now I can tell them without being burned. These truths do not have to be hurled in men's faces. They are not intended to ignite fervor. I do not trust fervor.

Every time it has burst out somewhere, it has brought fire, famine, misery. . . . And contempt for man.

Fervor is the weapon of choice of the impotent.

Of those who heat the iron in order to shape it at once. I should prefer to warm man's body and leave him. We might reach this result: mankind retaining this fire through self-combustion.

Mankind set free of the trampoline that is the resistance of others, and digging into its own flesh to find a meaning.

Only a few of those who read this book will understand the problems that were encountered in its composition.

In an age when skeptical doubt has taken root in the world, when in the words of a gang of *salauds* it is no longer possible to find the sense of non-sense, it becomes harder to penetrate to a level where the categories of sense and non-sense are not yet invoked.

The black man wants to be white. The white man slaves to reach a human level.

In the course of this essay we shall observe the development of an effort to understand the black-white relation.

The white man is sealed in his whiteness.

The black man in his blackness.

We shall seek to ascertain the directions of this dual narcissism and the motivations that inspire it.

At the beginning of my speculations it seems inappropriate to elaborate the conclusions that the reader will find.

Concern with the elimination of a vicious circle has been the only guide-line for my efforts.

There is a fact: White men consider themselves superior to black men.

There is another fact: Black men want to prove to white men, at all costs, the richness of their thought, the equal value of their intellect.

How do we extricate ourselves?

A moment ago I spoke of narcissism. Indeed, I believe that only a psychoanalytical interpretation of the black problem can lay bare the anomalies of affect that are responsible for the structure of the complex. I shall attempt a complete lysis of this morbid body. I believe that the individual should tend to take on the universality inherent in the human condition. And when I say this, I am thinking impartially of men like Gobineau or women like Mayotte Capécia. But, in order to arrive at this judgment, it is imperative to eliminate a whole set of defects left over from childhood.

Man's tragedy, Nietzsche said, is that he was once a child. None the less, we cannot afford to forget that, as Charles Odier has shown us, the neurotic's fate remains in his own hands.

However painful it may be for me to accept this conclusion, I am obliged to state it: For the black man there is only one destiny. And it is white.

Before beginning the case, I have to say certain things. The analysis that I am undertaking is psychological. In spite of this it is apparent to me that the effective disalienation of the black man entails an immediate recognition of social and economic realities. If there is an inferiority complex, it is the outcome of a double process:

—primarily, economic;

—subsequently, the internalization—or, better, the epidermalization—of this inferiority.

Reacting against the constitutionalist tendency of the late nineteenth century, Freud insisted that the individual factor be taken into account through psychoanalysis. He substituted for a phylogenetic theory the ontogenetic perspective. It will be seen that the black man's alienation is not an individual question. Beside phylogeny and ontogeny stands sociogeny. In one sense, conforming to the view of Leconte and Damey,[1] let us say that this is a question of a sociodiagnostic.

What is the prognosis?

But society, unlike biochemical processes, cannot escape human influences. Man is what brings society into being. The prognosis is in the hands of those who are willing to get rid of the worm-eaten roots of the structure.

The black man must wage his war on both levels: Since historically they influence each other, any unilateral liberation is incomplete, and the gravest mistake would be to believe in their automatic interdependence. Besides, such a systematic tendency is contrary to the facts. This will be proved.

Reality, for once, requires a total understanding. On the objective level as on the subjective level, a solution has to be supplied.

And to declare in the tone of "it's-all-my-fault" that what matters is the salvation of the soul is not worth the effort.

There will be an authentic disalienation only to the

1. M. Leconte and A. Damey, *Essai critique des nosographies psychiatriques actuelles.*

degree to which things, in the most materialistic meaning of the word, will have been restored to their proper places.

It is good form to introduce a work in psychology with a statement of its methodological point of view. I shall be derelict. I leave methods to the botanists and the mathematicians. There is a point at which methods devour themselves.

I should like to start from there. I shall try to discover the various attitudes that the Negro adopts in contact with white civilization.

The "jungle savage" is not what I have in mind. That is because for him certain factors have not yet acquired importance.

I believe that the fact of the juxtaposition of the white and black races has created a massive psychoexistential complex. I hope by analyzing it to destroy it.

Many Negroes will not find themselves in what follows.

This is equally true of many whites.

But the fact that I feel a foreigner in the worlds of the schizophrenic or the sexual cripple in no way diminishes their reality.

The attitudes that I propose to describe are real. I have encountered them innumerable times.

Among students, among workers, among the pimps of Pigalle or Marseille, I have been able to isolate the same components of aggressiveness and passivity.

This book is a clinical study. Those who recognize themselves in it, I think, will have made a step forward. I seriously hope to persuade my brother, whether black or white, to tear off with all his strength the shameful livery put together by centuries of incomprehension.

The architecture of this work is rooted in the temporal. Every human problem must be considered from the standpoint of time. Ideally, the present will always contribute to the building of the future.

And this future is not the future of the cosmos but rather the future of my century, my country, my existence. In no fashion should I undertake to prepare the world that will come later. I belong irreducibly to my time.

And it is for my own time that I should live. The future should be an edifice supported by living men. This structure is connected to the present to the extent that I consider the present in terms of something to be exceeded.

The first three chapters deal with the modern Negro. I take the black man of today and I try to establish his attitudes in the white world. The last two chapters are devoted to an attempt at a psychopathological and philosophical explanation of the *state of being* a Negro.

The analysis is, above all, regressive.

The fourth and fifth chapters rest on a fundamentally different basis.

In the fourth chapter I examine a work[2] that in my opinion is dangerous. The author, O. Mannoni, is, moreover, aware of the ambiguity of his position. That perhaps is one of the merits of his evidence. He has tried to account for a situation. It is our right to say that we are not satisfied. It is our duty to show the author how we differ from him.

The fifth chapter, which I have called *The Fact of Blackness,* is important for more than one reason. It portrays the Negro face to face with his race. It will be observed that there is no common link between the Negro

2. [Dominique] O. Mannoni, *Prospero and Caliban: The Psychology of Colonization* (New York, Praeger, 1964). Originally *Psychologie de la Colonisation* (Paris, Editions du Seuil, 1950).

of this chapter and the Negro who wants to go to bed with a white woman. In the latter there is clearly a wish to be white. A lust for revenge, in any case. Here, in contrast, we observe the desperate struggles of a Negro who is driven to discover the meaning of black identity. White civilization and European culture have forced an existential deviation on the Negro. I shall demonstrate elsewhere that what is often called the black soul is a white man's artifact.

The educated Negro, slave of the spontaneous and cosmic Negro myth, feels at a given stage that his race no longer understands him.

Or that he no longer understands it.

Then he congratulates himself on this, and enlarging the difference, the incomprehension, the disharmony, he finds in them the meaning of his real humanity. Or more rarely he wants to belong to his people. And it is with rage in his mouth and abandon in his heart that he buries himself in the vast black abyss. We shall see that this attitude, so heroically absolute, renounces the present and the future in the name of a mystical past.

Since I was born in the Antilles, my observations and my conclusions are valid only for the Antilles—at least concerning the black man *at home*. Another book could be dedicated to explaining the differences that separate the Negro of the Antilles from the Negro of Africa. Perhaps one day I shall write it. Perhaps too it will no longer be necessary—a fact for which we could only congratulate ourselves.

Chapter One

THE NEGRO AND LANGUAGE

I ascribe a basic importance to the phenomenon of language. That is why I find it necessary to begin with this subject, which should provide us with one of the elements in the colored man's comprehension of the dimension of *the other*. For it is implicit that to speak is to exist absolutely for the other.

The black man has two dimensions. One with his fellows, the other with the white man. A Negro behaves differently with a white man and with another Negro. That this self-division is a direct result of colonialist subjugation is beyond question. . . . No one would dream of doubting that its major artery is fed from the heart of those various theories that have tried to prove that the Negro is a stage in the slow evolution of monkey into man. Here is objective evidence that expresses reality.

But when one has taken cognizance of this situation, when one has understood it, one considers the job completed. How can one then be deaf to that voice rolling down the stages of history: "What matters is not to know the world but to change it."

This matters appallingly in our lifetime.

To speak means to be in a position to use a certain syntax, to grasp the morphology of this or that language, but it means above all to assume a culture, to support the weight of a civilization. Since the situation is not one-way only, the statement of it should reflect the fact. Here the reader is asked to concede certain points that, however unaceptable they may seem in the beginning, will find the measure of their validity in the facts.

The problem that we confront in this chapter is this: The Negro of the Antilles will be proportionately whiter—that is, he will come closer to being a real human being—in direct ratio to his mastery of the French language. I am not unaware that this is one of man's attitudes face to face with Being. A man who has a language consequently possesses the world expressed and implied by that language. What we are getting at becomes plain: Mastery of language affords remarkable power. Paul Valéry knew this, for he called language "the god gone astray in the flesh."[1]

In a work now in preparation I propose to investigate this phenomenon.[2] For the moment I want to show why the Negro of the Antilles, whoever he is, has always to face the problem of language. Furthermore, I will broaden the field of this description and through the Negro of the Antilles include every colonized man.

Every colonized people—in other words, every people in whose soul an inferiority complex has been created by the death and burial of its local cultural originality—finds itself face to face with the language of the civilizing nation; that is, with the culture of the mother country. The colonized is elevated above his jungle status in proportion to his adoption of the mother country's cultural standards. He becomes whiter as he renounces his blackness, his jungle. In the French colonial army, and particularly in the Senegalese regiments, the black officers serve

1. *Charmes* (Paris, Gallimard, 1952).
2. *Le langage et l'agressivité.*

first of all as interpreters. They are used to convey the master's orders to their fellows, and they too enjoy a certain position of honor.

There is the city, there is the country. There is the capital, there is the province. Apparently the problem in the mother country is the same. Let us take a Lyonnais in Paris: He boasts of the quiet of his city, the intoxicating beauty of the quays of the Rhône, the splendor of the plane trees, and all those other things that fascinate people who have nothing to do. If you meet him again when he has returned from Paris, and especially if you do not know the capital, he will never run out of its praises: Paris-city-of-light, the Seine, the little garden restaurants, know Paris and die. . . .

The process repeats itself with the man of Martinique. First of all on his island: Basse-Pointe, Marigot, Gros-Morne, and, opposite, the imposing Fort-de-France. Then, and this is the important point, beyond his island. The Negro who knows the mother country is a demigod. In this connection I offer a fact that must have struck my compatriots. Many of them, after stays of varying length in metropolitan France, go home to be deified. The most eloquent form of ambivalence is adopted toward them by the native, the-one-who-never-crawled-out-of-his-hole, the *bitaco*. The black man who has lived in France for a length of time returns radically changed. To express it in genetic terms, his phenotype undergoes a definitive, an absolute mutation.[3] Even before he had gone away, one could tell from the almost aerial manner of his carriage that new forces had been set in motion. When he met

---

3. By that I mean that Negroes who return to their original environments convey the impression that they have completed a cycle, that they have added to themselves something that was lacking. They return literally full of themselves.

a friend or an acquaintance, his greeting was no longer the wide sweep of the arm: With great reserve our "new man" bowed slightly. The habitually raucous voice hinted at a gentle inner stirring as of rustling breezes. For the Negro knows that over there in France there is a stereotype of him that will fasten on to him at the pier in Le Havre or Marseille: "Ah come fom Mahtinique, it's the fuhst time Ah've eveh come to Fance." He knows that what the poets call the *divine gurgling* (listen to Creole) is only a halfway house between pidgin-nigger and French. The middle class in the Antilles never speak Creole except to their servants. In school the children of Martinique are taught to scorn the dialect. One avoids *Creolisms.* Some families completely forbid the use of Creole, and mothers ridicule their children for speaking it.

> My mother wanting a son to keep in mind
> if you do not know your history lesson
> you will not go to mass on Sunday in
> your Sunday clothes
> that child will be a disgrace to the family
> that child will be our curse
> shut up I told you you must speak French
> the French of France
> the Frenchman's French
> French French[4]

Yes, I must take great pains with my speech, because I shall be more or less judged by it. With great contempt they will say of me, "He doesn't even know how to speak French."

In any group of young men in the Antilles, the one who expresses himself well, who has mastered the language,

4. Léon-G. Damas, "Hoquet," in *Pigments,* in Leopold S.-Senghor, ed., *Anthologie de la nouvelle poésie nègre et malgache* (Paris, Presses Universitaires de France, 1948), pp. 15-17.

is inordinately feared; keep an eye on that one, he is almost white. In France one says, "He talks like a book." In Martinique, "He talks like a white man."

The Negro arriving in France will react against the myth of the *R*-eating man from Martinique. He will become aware of it, and he will really go to war against it. He will practice not only rolling his *R* but embroidering it. Furtively observing the slightest reactions of others, listening to his own speech, suspicious of his own tongue—a wretchedly lazy organ—he will lock himself into his room and read aloud for hours—desperately determined to learn *diction*.

Recently an acquaintance told me a story. A Martinique Negro landed at Le Havre and went into a bar. With the utmost self-confidence he called, "Waite*rrr!* Bing me a beeya." Here is a genuine intoxication. Resolved not to fit the myth of the nigger-who-eats his-*R*'s, he had acquired a fine supply of them but allocated it badly.

There is a psychological phenomenon that consists in the belief that the world will open to the extent to which frontiers are broken down. Imprisoned on his island, lost in an atmosphere that offers not the slightest outlet, the Negro breathes in this appeal of Europe like pure air. For, it must be admitted, Aimé Césaire was generous—in his *Cahier d'un retour au pays natal*. This town of Fort-de-France is truly flat, stranded. Lying there naked to the sun, that "flat, sprawling city, stumbling over its own common sense, winded by its load of endlessly repeated crosses, pettish at its destiny, voiceless, thwarted in every direction, incapable of feeding on the juices of its soil, blocked, cut off, confined, divorced from fauna and flora."[5]

Césaire's description of it is anything but poetic. It is understandable, then, when at the news that he is getting

5. *Cahiers* (Paris, Présence Africaine, 1956), p. 30.

into France (quite like someone who, in the colloquial phrase, is "getting a start in life") the black man is jubilant and makes up his mind to change. There is no thematic pattern, however; his structure changes independently of any reflective process. In the United States there is a center directed by Pearce and Williamson; it is called Peckham. These authors have shown that in married couples a biochemical alteration takes place in the partners, and, it seems, they have discovered the presence of certain hormones in the husband of a pregnant woman. It would be equally interesting—and there are plenty of subjects for the study—to investigate the modifications of body fluids that occur in Negroes when they arrive in France. Or simply to study through tests the psychic changes both before they leave home and after they have spent a month in France.

What are by common consent called the human sciences have their own drama. Should one postulate a type for human reality and describe its psychic modalities only through deviations from it, or should one not rather strive unremittingly for a concrete and ever new understanding of man?

When one reads that after the age of twenty-nine a man can no longer love and that he must wait until he is forty-nine before his capacity for affect revives, one feels the ground give way beneath one. The only possibility of regaining one's balance is to face the whole problem, for all these discoveries, all these inquiries lead only in one direction: to make man admit that he is nothing, absolutely nothing—and that he must put an end to the narcissism on which he relies in order to imagine that he is different from the other "animals."

This amounts to nothing more nor less than *man's surrender*.

Having reflected on that, I grasp my narcissism with both hands and I turn my back on the degradation of those who would make man a mere mechanism. If there can be no discussion on a philosophical level—that is, the plane of the basic needs of human reality—I am willing to work on the psychoanalytical level—in other words, the level of the "failures," in the sense in which one speaks of engine failures.

The black man who arrives in France changes because to him the country represents the Tabernacle; he changes not only because it is from France that he received his knowledge of Montesquieu, Rousseau, and Voltaire, but also because France gave him his physicians, his department heads, his innumerable little functionaries—from the sergeant-major "fifteen years in the service" to the policeman who was born in Panissières. There is a kind of magic vault of distance, and the man who is leaving next week for France creates round himself a magic circle in which the words *Paris, Marseille, Sorbonne, Pigalle* become the keys to the vault. He leaves for the pier, and the amputation of his being diminishes as the silhouette of his ship grows clearer. In the eyes of those who have come to see him off he can read the evidence of his own mutation, his power. "Good-by bandanna, good-by straw hat. . . ."

Now that we have got him to the dock, let him sail; we shall see him again. For the moment, let us go to welcome one of those who are coming home. The "newcomer" reveals himself at once; he answers only in French, and often he no longer understands Creole. There is a relevant illustration in folklore. After several months of living in France, a country boy returns to his family. Noticing a farm implement, he asks his father, an old don't-pull-that-kind-of-thing-on-me peasant, "Tell me, what does one call that apparatus?" His father replies by dropping the tool on the boy's feet, and the amnesia vanishes. Remarkable therapy.

There is the newcomer, then. He no longer understands the dialect, he talks about the Opéra, which he may never have seen except from a distance, but above all he adopts a critical attitude toward his compatriots. Confronted with the most trivial occurrence, he becomes an oracle. He is the one who knows. He betrays himself in his speech. At the Savannah, where the young men of Fort-de-France spend their leisure, the spectacle is revealing: Everyone immediately waits for the newcomer to speak. As soon as the school day ends, they all go to the Savannah. This Savannah seems to have its own poetry. Imagine a square about 600 feet long and 125 feet wide, its sides bounded by worm-eaten tamarind trees, one end marked by the huge war memorial (the nation's gratitude to its children), the other by the Central Hotel; a miserable tract of uneven cobbles, pebbles that roll away under one's feet; and, amid all this, three or four hundred young fellows walking up and down, greeting one another, grouping—no, they never form groups, they go on walking.

"How's it going?"

"O.K. How's it with you?"

"O.K."

And that goes on for fifty years. Yes, this city is deplorably played out. So is its life.

They meet and talk. And if the newcomer soon gets the floor, it is because they were *waiting for him.* First of all to observe his manner: The slightest departure is seized on, picked apart, and in less than forty-eight hours it has been retailed all over Fort-de-France. There is no forgiveness when one who claims a superiority falls below the standard. Let him say, for instance, "It was not my good fortune, when in France, to observe mounted policemen," and he is done for. Only one choice remains to him: throw off his "Parisianism" or die of ridicule. For there is also no forgetting: When he marries, his wife will be aware that she is marrying a joke, and his children will have a legend to face and to live down.

What is the origin of this personality change? What is the source of this new way of being? Every dialect is a way of thinking, Damourette and Pichon said. And the fact that the newly returned Negro adopts a language different from that of the group into which he was born is evidence of a dislocation, a separation. Professor D. Westermann, in *The African Today* (p. 331), says that the Negroes' inferiority complex is particularly intensified among the most educated, who must struggle with it unceasingly. Their way of doing so, he adds, is frequently naïve: "The wearing of European clothes, whether rags or the most up-to-date style; using European furniture and European forms of social intercourse; adorning the Native language with European expressions; using bombastic phrases in speaking or writing a European language; all these contribute to a feeling of equality with the European and his achievements."

On the basis of other studies and my own personal observations, I want to try to show why the Negro adopts such a position, peculiar to him, with respect to European languages. Let me point out once more that the conclusions I have reached pertain to the French Antilles; at the same time, I am not unaware that the same behavior patterns obtain in every race that has been subjected to colonization.

I have known—and unfortunately I still know—people born in Dahomey or the Congo who pretend to be natives of the Antilles; I have known, and I still know, Antilles

Negroes who are annoyed when they are suspected of being Senegalese. This is because the Antilles Negro is more "civilized" than the African, that is, he is closer to the white man; and this difference prevails not only in back streets and on boulevards but also in public service and the army. Any Antilles Negro who performed his military service in a Senegalese infantry regiment is familiar with this disturbing climate: On one side he has the Europeans, whether born in his own country or in France, and on the other he has the Senegalese. I remember a day when, in the midst of combat, we had to wipe out a machine-gun nest. The Senegalese were ordered to attack three times, and each time they were forced back. Then one of them wanted to know why the *toubabs*[6] did not go into action. At such times, one no longer knows whether one is *toubab* or "native." And yet many Antilles Negroes see nothing to upset them in such European identification; on the contrary, they find it altogether normal. That would be all we need, to be taken for niggers! The Europeans despise the Senegalese, and the Antilles Negro rules the black roost as its unchallenged master. Admittedly as an extreme example, I offer a detail that is at least amusing. I was talking recently with someone from Martinique who told me with considerable resentment that some Guadeloupe Negroes were trying to "pass" as Martinicans. But, he added, the lie was rapidly discovered, because they are more savage than we are; which, again, means they are farther away from the white man. It is said that the Negro loves to jabber; in my own case, when I think of the word *jabber* I see a gay group of children calling and shouting for the sake of calling and shouting—children in the midst

6. Literally, this dialect word means *European;* by extension it was applied to any officer. (Translator's note.)

of play, to the degree to which play can be considered an initiation into life. The Negro loves to jabber, and from this theory it is not a long road that leads to a new proposition: The Negro is just a child. The psychoanalysts have a fine start here, and the term *orality* is soon heard.

But we have to go farther. The problem of language is too basic to allow us to hope to state it all here. Piaget's remarkable studies have taught us to distinguish the various stages in the mastery of language, and Gelb and Goldstein have shown us that the function of language is also broken into periods and steps. What interests us here is the black man confronted by the French language. We are trying to understand why the Antilles Negro is so fond of speaking French.

Jean-Paul Sartre, in *Orphée Noir,* which prefaces the *Anthology de la nouvelle poésie nègre et malgache,* tells us that the black poet will turn against the French language; but that does not apply in the Antilles. Here I share the opinion of Michel Leiris, who, discussing Creole, wrote not so long ago:

> Even now, despite the fact that it is a language that everyone knows more or less, though only the illiterate use it to the exclusion of French, Creole seems already predestined to become a relic eventually, once public education (however slow its progress, impeded by the insufficiency of school facilities everywhere, the paucity of reading matter available to the public, and the fact that the physical scale of living is often too low) has become common enough among the disinherited classes of the population.

And, the author adds:

> In the case of the poets that I am discussing here, there is no question of their deliberately becoming "Antilleans"—on the Provençal picturesque model—by employing a dead language which, furthermore, is utterly devoid of all ex-

ternal radiance regardless of its intrinsic qualities; it is rather a matter of their asserting, in opposition to white men filled with the worst racial prejudices, whose arrogance is more and more plainly demonstrated to be unfounded, the integrity of their personalities.[7]

If there is, for instance, a Gilbert Gratiant who writes in dialect, it must be admitted that he is a rarity. Let us point out, furthermore, that the poetic merit of such creation is quite dubious. There are, in contrast, real works of art translated from the Peul and Wolof dialects of Senegal, and I have found great interest in following the linguistic studies of Sheik Anta Diop.

Nothing of the sort in the Antilles. The language spoken officially is French; teachers keep a close watch over the children to make sure they do not use Creole. Let us not mention the ostensible reasons. It would seem, then, that the problem is this: In the Antilles, as in Brittany, there is a dialect and there is the French language. But this is false, for the Bretons do not consider themselves inferior to the French people. The Bretons have not been civilized by the white man.

By refusing to multiply our elements, we take the risk of not setting a limit to our field; for it is essential to convey to the black man that an attitude of rupture has never saved anyone. While it is true that I have to throw off an attacker who is strangling me, because I literally cannot breathe, the fact remains solely on the physiological foundation. To the mechanical problem of respiration it would be unsound to graft a psychological element, the impossibility of expansion.

What is there to say? Purely and simply this: When a bachelor of philosophy from the Antilles refuses to apply

7. "Martinique-Guadeloupe-Haiti," *Les Temps Modernes,* February, 1950, p. 1347.

for certification as a teacher on the ground of his color, I say that philosophy has never saved anyone. When someone else strives and strains to prove to me that black men are as intelligent as white men, I say that intelligence has never saved anyone; and that is true, for, if philosophy and intelligence are invoked to proclaim the equality of men, they have also been employed to justify the extermination of men.

Before going any farther I find it necessary to say certain things. I am speaking here, on the one hand, of alienated (duped) blacks, and, on the other, of no less alienated (duping and duped) whites. If one hears a Sartre or a Cardinal Verdier declare that the outrage of the color problem has survived far too long, one can conclude only that their position is normal. Anyone can amass references and quotations to prove that "color prejudice" is indeed an imbecility and an iniquity that must be eliminated.

Sartre begins *Orphée Noir* thus: "What then did you expect when you unbound the gag that had muted those black mouths? That they would chant your praises? Did you think that when those heads that our fathers had forcibly bowed down to the ground were raised again, you would find adoration in their eyes?"[8] I do not know; but I say that he who looks into my eyes for anything but a perpetual question will have to lose his sight; neither recognition nor hate. And if I cry out, it will not be a black cry. No, from the point of view adopted here, there is no black problem. Or at any rate if there is one it concerns the whites only accidentally. It is a story that takes place in darkness, and the sun that is carried within me must shine into the smallest crannies.

8. Jean-Paul Sartre, *Orphée Noir,* in *Anthologie de la nouvelle poésie nègre et malgache,* p. ix.

Dr. H. L. Gordon, attending physician at the Mathari Mental Hospital in Nairobi, declared in an article in *The East African Medical Journal* (1943): "A highly technical skilled examination of a series of 100 brains of normal Natives has found naked eye and microscopic facts indicative of inherent new brain inferiority. . . . Quantitatively," he added, "the inferiority amounts to 14.8 percent."[9]

It has been said that the Negro is the link between monkey and man—meaning, of course, white man. And only on page 108 of his book does Sir Alan Burns come to the conclusion that "we are unable to accept as scientifically proved the theory that the black man is inherently inferior to the white, or that he comes from a different stock. . . ." Let me add that it would be easy to prove the absurdity of statements such as this: "It is laid down in the Bible that the separation of the white and black races will be continued in heaven as on earth, and those blacks who are admitted into the Kingdom of Heaven will find themselves separately lodged in certain of those many mansions of Our Father that are mentioned in the New Testament." Or this: "We are the chosen people—look at the color of our skins. The others are black or yellow: That is because of their sins."

Ah, yes, as you can see, by calling on humanity, on the belief in dignity, on love, on charity, it would be easy to prove, or to win the admission, that the black is the equal of the white. But my purpose is quite different: What I want to do is help the black man to free himself of the arsenal of complexes that has been developed by the colonial environment. M. Achille, who teaches at the Lycée du Parc in Lyon, once during a lecture told of a

9. Quoted in Sir Alan Burns, *Colour Prejudice* (London, Allen & Unwin, 1948), p. 101.

personal experience. It is a universally known experience. It is a rare Negro living in France who cannot duplicate it. Being a Catholic, Achille took part in a student pilgrimage. A priest, observing the black face in his flock, said to him, "You go 'way big Savannah what for and come 'long us?" Very politely Achille gave him a truthful answer, and it was not the young fugitive from the Savannah who came off the worse. Everyone laughed at the exchange and the pilgrimage proceeded. But if we stop right here, we shall see that the fact that the priest spoke pidgin-nigger leads to certain observations:

1. "Oh, I know the blacks. They must be spoken to kindly; talk to them about their country; it's all in knowing how to talk to them. For instance. . . ." I am not at all exaggerating: A white man addressing a Negro behaves exactly like an adult with a child and starts smirking, whispering, patronizing, cozening. It is not one white man I have watched, but hundreds; and I have not limited my investigation to any one class but, if I may claim an essentially objective position, I have made a point of observing such behavior in physicians, policemen, employers. I shall be told, by those who overlook my purpose, that I should have directed my attention elsewhere, that there are white men who do not fit my description.

To these objections I reply that the subject of our study is the dupes and those who dupe them, the alienated, and that if there are white men who behave naturally when they meet Negroes, they certainly do not fall within the scope of our examination. If my patient's liver is functioning as it should, I am not going to take it for granted that his kidneys are sound. Having found the liver normal, I leave it to its normality, which is normal, and turn my attention to the kidneys: As it happens, the kidneys are diseased. Which means simply that, side by side with normal people who behave naturally in accordance with a human psychology, there are others who behave pathologically in accordance with an inhuman psychology. And it happens that the existence of men of this sort has determined a certain number of realities to the elimination of which I should like to contribute here.

Talking to Negroes in this way gets down to their level, it puts them at ease, it is an effort to make them understand us, it reassures them. . . .

The physicians of the public health services know this very well. Twenty European patients, one after another, come in: "Please sit down. . . . Why do you wish to consult me? . . . What are your symptoms? . . ." Then comes a Negro or an Arab: "Sit there, boy. . . . What's bothering you? . . . Where does it hurt, huh? . . ." When, that is, they do not say: "You not feel good, no?"

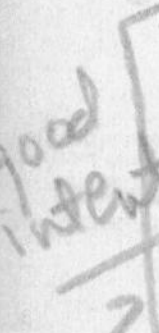

2. To speak pidgin to a Negro makes him angry, because he himself is a pidgin-nigger-talker. But, I will be told, there is no wish, no intention to anger him. I grant this; but it is just this absence of wish, this lack of interest, this indifference, this automatic manner of classifying him, imprisoning him, primitivizing him, decivilizing him, that makes him angry.

If a man who speaks pidgin to a man of color or an Arab does not see anything wrong or evil in such behavior, it is because he has never stopped to think. I myself have been aware, in talking to certain patients, of the exact instant at which I began to slip. . . .

Examining this seventy-three-year-old farm woman, whose mind was never strong and who is now far gone in dementia, I am suddenly aware of the collapse of the *antennae* with which I touch and through which I am touched. The fact that I adopt a language suitable to dementia, to feeble-mindedness; the fact that I "talk down" to this poor woman of seventy-three; the fact that I condescend to her in my quest for a diagnosis, are the stigmata of a dereliction in my relations with other people.

What an idealist, people will say. Not at all: It is just that the others are scum. I make it a point always to talk to the so-called *bicots*[10] in normal French, and I have always been understood. They answer me as well as their varying means permit; but I will not allow myself to resort to paternalistic "understanding."

"G'morning, pal. Where's it hurt? Huh? Lemme see—belly ache? Heart pain?"

With that indefinable tone that the hacks in the free clinics have mastered so well.

One feels perfectly justified when the patient answers in the same fashion. "You see? I wasn't kidding you. That's just the way they are."

When the opposite occurs, one must retract one's pseudopodia and behave like a man. The whole structure crumbles. A black man who says to you: "I am in no sense your boy, Monsieur. . . ." Something new under the sun.

But one must go lower. You are in a bar, in Rouen or Strasbourg, and you have the misfortune to be spotted by an old drunk. He sits down at your table right off. "You—Africa? Dakar, Rufisque, whorehouse, dames, café, mangoes, bananas. . . ." You stand up and leave, and your farewell is a torrent of abuse: "You didn't play big shot like that in your jungle, you dirty nigger!"

Mannoni has described what he calls the Prospero complex. We shall come back to these discoveries, which will make it possible for us to understand the psychology of

10. Vulgar French for *Arab*. (Translator's note.)

colonialism. But we can already state that to talk pidgin-nigger is to express this thought: "You'd better keep your place."

I meet a Russian or a German who speaks French badly. With gestures I try to give him the information that he requests, but at the same time I can hardly forget that he has a language of his own, a country, and that perhaps he is a lawyer or an engineer there. In any case, he is foreign to my group, and his standards must be different.

When it comes to the case of the Negro, nothing of the kind. He has no culture, no civilization, no "long historical past."

This may be the reason for the strivings of contemporary Negroes: to prove the existence of a black civilization to the white world at all costs.

Willy-nilly, the Negro has to wear the livery that the white man has sewed for him. Look at children's picture magazines: Out of every Negro mouth comes the ritual "Yassuh, boss." It is even more remarkable in motion pictures. Most of the American films for which French dialogue is dubbed in offer the type-Negro: "Sho' good!"

In one of these recent films, *Requins d'acier*, one character was a Negro crewman in a submarine who talked in the most classic dialect imaginable. What is more, he was all *nigger*, walking backward, shaking at the slightest sign of irritation on the part of a petty officer; ultimately he was killed in the course of the voyage. Yet I am convinced that the original dialogue did not resort to the same means of expression. And, even if it did, I can see no reason why, in a democratic France that includes sixty million citizens of color, dubbing must repeat every stupidity that crosses the ocean. It is because the Negro has to be shown in a certain way; and from the Negro in *Sans Pitié*—"Me work hard, me never lie, me never steal"

—to the servant girl of *Duel in the Sun* one meets the same stereotype.

Yes, the black man is supposed to be a good nigger; once this has been laid down, the rest follows of itself. To make him talk pidgin is to fasten him to the effigy of him, to snare him, to imprison him, the eternal victim of an essence, of an *appearance* for which he is not responsible. And naturally, just as a Jew who spends money without thinking about it is suspect, a black man who quotes Montesquieu had better be watched. Please understand me: watched in the sense that he is starting something. Certainly I do not contend that the black student is suspect to his fellows or to his teachers. But outside university circles there is an army of fools: What is important is not to educate them, but to teach the Negro not to be the slave of their archetypes.

That these imbeciles are the product of a psychological-economic system I will grant. But that does not get us much farther along.

When a Negro talks of Marx, the first reaction is always the same: "We have brought you up to our level and now you turn against your benefactors. Ingrates! Obviously nothing can be expected of you." And then too there is that bludgeon argument of the plantation-owner in Africa: Our enemy is the teacher.

What I am asserting is that the European has a fixed concept of the Negro, and there is nothing more exasperating than to be asked: "How long have you been in France? You speak French so well."

It can be argued that people say this because many Negroes speak pidgin. But that would be too easy. You are on a train and you ask another passenger: "I beg your pardon, sir, would you mind telling me where the dining-car is?"

"Sure, fella. You go out door, see, go corridor, you go straight, go one car, go two car, go three car, you there."

No, speaking pidgin-nigger closes off the black man; it perpetuates a state of conflict in which the white man injects the black with extremely dangerous foreign bodies. Nothing is more astonishing than to hear a black man express himself properly, for then in truth he is putting on the white world. I have had occasion to talk with students of foreign origin. They speak French badly: Little Crusoe, alias Prospero, is at ease then. He explains, informs, interprets, helps them with their studies. But with a Negro he is completely baffled; the Negro has made himself just as knowledgeable. With him this game cannot be played, he is a complete replica of the white man. So there is nothing to do but to give in.[11]

After all that has just been said, it will be understood that the first impulse of the black man is to say *no* to those who attempt to build a definition of him. It is understandable that the first action of the black man is a *reaction*, and, since the Negro is appraised in terms of the extent of his assimilation, it is also understandable why the newcomer expresses himself only in French. It is because he wants to emphasize the rupture that has now occurred. He is incarnating a new type of man that he imposes on his associates and his family. And so his old mother can no

11. "I knew some Negroes in the School of Medicine . . . in a word, they were a disappointment; the color of their skin should have permitted them to give *us* the opportunity to be charitable, generous, or scientifically friendly. They were derelict in this duty, this claim on our good will. All our tearful tenderness, all our calculated solicitude were a drug on the market. We had no Negroes to condescend to, nor did we have anything to hate them for; they counted for virtually as much as we in the scale of the little jobs and petty chicaneries of daily life." Michel Salomon, "D'un juif à des nègres," *Présence Africaine*, No. 5, p. 776.

longer understand him when he talks to her about his *duds,* the family's *crummy joint,* the *dump* . . . all of it, of course, tricked out with the appropriate accent.

In every country of the world there are climbers, "the ones who forget who they are," and, in contrast to them, "the ones who remember where they came from." The Antilles Negro who goes home from France expresses himself in dialect if he wants to make it plain that nothing has changed. One can feel this at the dock where his family and his friends are waiting for him. Waiting for him not only because he is physically arriving, but in the sense of waiting for the chance to strike back. They need a minute or two in order to make their diagnosis. If the voyager tells his acquaintances, "I am so happy to be back with you. Good Lord, it is hot in this country, I shall certainly not be able to endure it very long," they know: A European has got off the ship.

In a more limited group, when students from the Antilles meet in Paris, they have the choice of two possibilities:

—either to stand with the white world (that is to say, the real world), and, since they will speak French, to be able to confront certain problems and incline to a certain degree of universality in their conclusions;

—or to reject Europe, "Yo,"[12] and cling together in their dialect, making themselves quite comfortable in what we shall call the *Umwelt* of Martinique; by this I mean—and this applies particularly to my brothers of the Antilles—that when one of us tries, in Paris or any other university city, to study a problem seriously, he is accused of self-aggrandizement, and the surest way of cutting him

12. A generic term for *other people,* applied especially to Europeans.

down is to remind him of the Antilles by exploding into dialect. This must be recognized as one of the reasons why so many friendships collapse after a few months of life in Europe.

My theme being the disalienation of the black man, I want to make him feel that whenever there is a lack of understanding between him and his fellows in the presence of the white man there is a lack of judgment.

A Senegalese learns Creole in order to pass as an Antilles native: I call this alienation.

The Antilles Negroes who know him never weary of making jokes about him: I call this a lack of judgment.

It becomes evident that we were not mistaken in believing that a study of the language of the Antilles Negro would be able to show us some characteristics of his world. As I said at the start, there is a retaining-wall relation between language and group.

To speak a language is to take on a world, a culture. The Antilles Negro who wants to be white will be the whiter as he gains greater mastery of the cultural tool that language is. Rather more than a year ago in Lyon, I remember, in a lecture I had drawn a parallel between Negro and European poetry, and a French acquaintance told me enthusiastically, "At bottom you are a white man." The fact that I had been able to investigate so interesting a problem through the white man's language gave me honorary citizenship.

Historically, it must be understood that the Negro wants to speak French because it is the key that can open doors which were still barred to him fifty years ago. In the Antilles Negro who comes within this study we find a quest for subtleties, for refinements of language—so many further means of proving to himself that he has measured up to the culture.[13] It has been said that the orators of the Antilles have a gift of eloquence that would leave any European breathless. I am reminded of a relevant story: In the election campaign of 1945, Aimé Césaire, who was seeking a deputy's seat, addressed a large audience in the boys' school in Fort-de-France. In the middle of his speech a woman fainted. The next day, an acquaintance told me about this, and commented: "*Français a té tellement chaud que la femme là tombé malcadi.*[14] The power of language!

Some other facts are worth a certain amount of attention: for example, Charles-André Julien introducing Aimé Césaire as "a Negro poet with a university degree," or again, quite simply, the expression, "a great black poet."

These ready-made phrases, which seem in a commonsense way to fill a need—for Aimé Césaire is really black and a poet—have a hidden subtlety, a permanent rub. I know nothing of Jean Paulhan except that he writes very interesting books; I have no idea how old Roger Caillois is, since the only evidences I have of his existence are the books of his that streak across my horizon. And let no one accuse me of affective allergies; what I am trying to say is that there is no reason why André Breton should say of Césaire, "Here is a black man who handles the French language as no white man today can."[15]

---

13. Compare for example the almost incredible store of anecdotes to which the election of any candidate gives rise. A filthy newspaper called the *Canard Déchaîné* could not get its fill of overwhelming Monsieur B. with devastating Creolisms. This is indeed the bludgeon of the Antilles: *He can't express himself in French.*

14. "*Le français (l'élégance de la forme) était tellement chaud que la femme est tombée en transes*" [His French (the refinement of his style) was so exciting that the woman swooned away].

15. Introduction to *Cahier d'un retour au pays natal*, p. 14.

And, even though Breton may be stating a fact, I do not see why there should be any paradox, anything to underline, for in truth M. Aimé Césaire is a native of Martinique and a university graduate.

Again we find this in Michel Leiris:

> If in the writers of the Antilles there does exist a desire to break away from the literary forms associated with formal education, such a desire, oriented toward a purer future, could not take on an aspect of folklore. Seeking above all, in literature, to formulate the message that is properly theirs, and in the case of some of them at least, to be the spokesmen of an authentic race whose potentials have never been acknowledged, they scorn such devices. Their intellectual growth took place almost exclusively within the framework of the French language, and it would be artifice for them to resort to a mode of speech that they virtually never use now except as something learned.[16]

But we should be honored, the blacks will reproach me, that a white man like Breton writes such things.

Let us go on. . . .

---

16. Michel Leiris, *op. cit*

Chapter Two

THE WOMAN OF COLOR AND THE WHITE MAN

Man is motion toward the world and toward his like. A movement of aggression, which leads to enslavement or to conquest; a movement of love, a gift of self, the ultimate stage of what by common accord is called ethical orientation. Every consciousness seems to have the capacity to demonstrate these two components, simultaneously or alternatively. The person I love will strengthen me by endorsing my assumption of my manhood, while the need to earn the admiration or the love of others will erect a value-making superstructure on my whole vision of the world.

In reaching an understanding of phenomena of this sort, the analyst and the phenomenologist are given a difficult task. And, if a Sartre has appeared to formulate a description of love as frustration, his *Being and Nothingness* amounting only to an analysis of dishonesty and inauthenticity, the fact remains that true, authentic love—wishing for others what one postulates for oneself, when that postulation unites the permanent values of human reality—entails the mobilization of psychic drives basically freed of unconscious conflicts.

Left far, far behind, the last *sequelae* of a titanic struggle carried on against *the other* have been dissipated.

Today I believe in the possibility of love; that is why I endeavor to trace its imperfections, its perversions.

In this chapter devoted to the relations between the woman of color and the European, it is our problem to ascertain to what extent authentic love will remain unattainable before one has purged oneself of that feeling of inferiority or that Adlerian exaltation, that overcompensation, which seem to be the indices of the black *Weltanschauung*.

For after all we have a right to be perturbed when we read, in *Je suis Martiniquaise*: "I should have liked to be married, but to a white man. But a woman of color is never altogether respectable in a white man's eyes. Even when he loves her. I knew that."[1] This passage, which serves in a way as the conclusion of a vast delusion, prods one's brain. One day a woman named Mayotte Capécia, obeying a motivation whose elements are difficult to detect, sat down to write 202 pages—her life—in which the most ridiculous ideas proliferated at random. The enthusiastic reception that greeted this book in certain circles forces us to analyze it. For me, all circumlocution is impossible: *Je suis Martiniquaise* is cut-rate merchandise, a sermon in praise of corruption.

Mayotte loves a white man to whom she submits in everything. He is her lord. She asks nothing, demands nothing, except a bit of whiteness in her life. When she tries to determine in her own mind whether the man is handsome or ugly, she writes, "All I know is that he had blue eyes, blond hair, and a light skin, and that I loved him." It is not difficult to see that a rearrangement of these elements in their proper hierarchy would produce

1. Mayotte Capécia, *Je suis Martiniquaise* (Paris, Corréa, 1948), p. 202.

something of this order: "I loved him because he had blue eyes, blond hair, and a light skin." We who come from the Antilles know one thing only too well: Blue eyes, the people say, frighten the Negro.

When I observed in my introduction that, historically, inferiority has been felt economically, I was hardly mistaken.

> There were evenings, unhappily, when he had to leave me alone in order to fulfill his social obligations. He would go to Didier, the fashionable part of Fort-de-France inhabited by the "Martinique whiteys," who are perhaps not too pure racially but who are often very rich (it is understood that one is white above a certain financial level), and the "France whiteys," most of them government people and military officers.
>
> Among André's colleagues, who like him had been marooned in the Antilles by the war, some had managed to have their wives join them. I understood that André could not always hold himself aloof from them. I also accepted the fact that I was barred from this society because I was a woman of color; but I could not help being jealous. It was no good his explaining to me that his private life was something that belonged to him alone and that his social and military life was something else, which was not within his control; I nagged so much that one day he took me to Didier. We spent the evening in one of those little villas that I had admired since my childhood, with two officers and their wives. The women kept watching me with a condescension that I found unbearable. I felt that I was wearing too much makeup, that I was not properly dressed, that I was not doing André credit, perhaps simply because of the color of my skin—in short, I spent so miserable an evening that I decided I would never again ask André to take me with him.[2]

---

2. *Ibid.*, p. 150.

It was Didier, the preserve of the richest people in Martinique, that magnetized all the girl's wishes. And she makes the point herself: One is white above a certain financial level. The houses in this section had long dazzled the lady. I have the feeling, however, that Mayotte Capécia is laying it on: She tells us that she did not go to Fort-de-France until she was grown, at about the age of eighteen; and yet the mansions of Didier had beguiled her childhood. There is an inconsistency here that becomes understandable when one grasps the background. It is in fact customary in Martinique to dream of a form of salvation that consists of magically turning white. A house in Didier, acceptance into that high society (Didier is on a hill that dominates the city), and there you have Hegel's subjective certainty made flesh. And in another way it is quite easy to see the place that the dialectic of being and having[3] would occupy in a description of this behavior. Such, however, is not the case with Mayotte. She is looked at with distaste. Things begin their usual course. . . . It is because she is a woman of color that she is not accepted in this society. Her resentment feeds on her own artificiality. We shall see why love is beyond the reach of the Mayotte Capécias of all nations. For the beloved should not allow me to turn my infantile fantasies into reality: On the contrary, he should help me to go beyond them. The childhood of Mayotte Capécia shows us a certain number of characteristics that illustrate the line of orientation she follows as an adult. And each time there is a movement or a contact, it will have a direct relation to her goal. It would seem indeed that for her white and black represent the two poles of a world, two poles in perpetual conflict: a genuinely Manichean con-

3. Gabriel Marcel, *Être et Avoir* (Paris, Aubier, 1935).

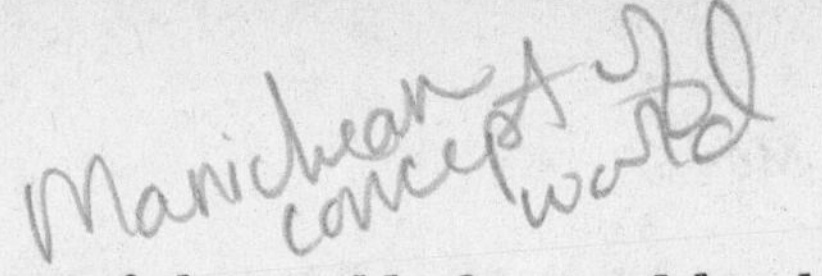

cept of the world; the word has been spoken, it must be remembered—white or black, that is the question.

I am white: that is to say that I possess beauty and virtue, which have never been black. I am the color of the daylight. . . .

I am black: I am the incarnation of a complete fusion with the world, an intuitive understanding of the earth, an abandonment of my ego in the heart of the cosmos, and no white man, no matter how intelligent he may be, can ever understand Louis Armstrong and the music of the Congo. If I am black, it is not the result of a curse, but it is because, having offered my skin, I have been able to absorb all the cosmic *effluvia*. I am truly a ray of sunlight under the earth. . . .

And there one lies body to body with one's blackness or one's whiteness, in full narcissistic cry, each sealed into his own peculiarity—with, it is true, now and then a flash or so, but these are threatened at their source.

From the first this is how the problem appears to Mayotte—at the fifth year of her age and the third page of her book: "She took her inkwell out of the desk and emptied it over his head." This was her own way of turning whites into blacks. But she quite soon recognized the futility of such attempts; and then there were Loulouze and her mother, who told her that life was difficult for a woman of color. So, since she could no longer try to blacken, to negrify the world, she was going to try, in her own body and in her own mind, to bleach it. To start, she would become a laundress: "I charged high prices, higher than elsewhere, but I worked better, and since people in Fort-de-France like their linens clean, they came to me. In the end, they were proud to have their laundry done by Mayotte."[4]

4. Capécia, *op. cit.*, p. 131.

I am sorry that Mayotte Capécia has told us nothing about her dreams. That would have made it easier to reach her unconscious. Instead of recognizing her absolute blackness, she proceeds to turn it into an accident. She learns that her grandmother was white.

> I found that I was proud of it. I was certainly not the only one who had white blood, but a white grandmother was not so ordinary as a white grandfather.[5] So my mother, then,

5. Since he is the master and more simply the male, the white man can allow himself the luxury of sleeping with many women. This is true in every country and especially in colonies. But when a white woman accepts a black man there is automatically a romantic aspect. It is a giving, not a seizing. In the colonies, in fact, even though there is little marriage or actual sustained cohabitation between whites and blacks, the number of hybrids is amazing. This is because the white men often sleep with their black servants. None the less, that does not provide any foundation for this passage from Mannoni:

> Thus one part of our drives would quite naturally impel us toward the most alien types. That is no mere literary illusion; there was no question of literature, and the illusion was probably very slight when Galliéni's soldiers chose young *ramatoa* as their more or less temporary wives. In fact these first contacts presented no difficulties at all. This was in part due to the healthy sex life of the Malagasies, which was unmarred by complexes. But this only goes to show that racial conflicts develop gradually and do not arise spontaneously. (*Prospero and Caliban*, p. 112).

Let us not exaggerate. When a soldier of the conquering army went to bed with a young Malagasy girl, there was undoubtedly no tendency on his part to respect her entity as another person. The racial conflicts did not come later, they coexisted. The fact that Algerian colonists go to bed with their fourteen-year-old housemaids in no way demonstrates a lack of racial conflicts in Algeria. No, the problem is more complicated. And Mayotte Capécia is right: It is an honor to be the daughter of a white woman. That proves that one was not "made in the bushes." (This expression is applied exclusively to all the illegitimate children of the upper class in

was a mixture? I should have guessed it when I looked at her light color. I found her prettier than ever, and cleverer, and more refined. If she had married a white man, do you suppose I should have been completely white? . . . And life might not have been so hard for me? . . . I daydreamed about this grandmother whom I had never known and who had died because she had loved a colored man of Martinique. . . . How could a Canadian woman have loved a man of Martinique? I could never stop thinking of our priest, and I made up my mind that I could never love anyone but a white man, a blue-eyed blonde, a Frenchman.[6]

We are thus put on notice that what Mayotte wants is a kind of lactification. For, in a word, the race must be whitened; every woman in Martinique knows this, says it, repeats it. Whiten the race, save the race, but not in the sense that one might think: not "preserve the uniqueness of that part of the world in which they grew up," but make sure that it will be white. Every time I have made up my mind to analyze certain kinds of behavior, I have been unable to avoid the consideration of certain nauseating phenomena. The number of sayings, proverbs, petty rules of conduct that govern the choice of a lover in the Antilles is astounding. It is always essential to avoid falling back into the pit of niggerhood, and every woman in the Antilles, whether in a casual flirtation or in a serious affair, is determined to select the least black of the men. Sometimes, in order to justify a bad investment, she is compelled to resort to such arguments as this: "X is black, but misery is blacker." I know a great number of girls from Martinique, students in France, who admitted to me with complete candor—completely white candor—that they would find it impossible to marry

---

Martinique; they are known to be extremely numerous: Aubery, for example, is supposed to have fathered almost fifty.)

6. Capécia, *op. cit.*, p. 59.

black men. (Get out of that and then deliberately go back to it? Thank you, no.) Besides, they added, it is not that we deny that blacks have any good qualities, but you know it is so much better to be white. I was talking only recently to one such woman. Breathless with anger, she stormed at me, "If Césaire makes so much display about accepting his race, it is because he really feels it as a curse. Do the whites boast like that about theirs? Every one of us has a white potential, but some try to ignore it and others simply reverse it. As far as I am concerned, I wouldn't marry a Negro for anything in the world." Such attitudes are not rare, and I must confess that they disturb me, for in a few years this young woman will have finished her examinations and gone off to teach in some school in the Antilles. It is not hard to guess what will come of that.

An enormous task confronts the Antillean who has begun by carefully examining the objectivity of the various prejudices prevailing in his environment. When I began this book, having completed my medical studies, I thought of presenting it as my thesis. But dialectic required the constant adoption of positions. Although I had more or less concentrated on the psychic alienation of the black man, I could not remain silent about certain things which, however psychological they may be, produce consequences that extend into the domains of other sciences.

Every experience, especially if it turns out to be sterile, has to become a component of reality and thus play a part in the restructuring of reality. That is to say that the patriarchal European family with its flaws, its failures, its vices, closely linked to the society that we know, produces about 30 per cent neurotics. The problem is to create, with the help of psychoanalytical, sociological, political lessons, a new family environment capable of reducing, if not of eliminating, the proportion of waste, in the asocial sense of the word.

In other words, the question is whether *basic personality* is a constant or a variable.

All these frantic women of color in quest of white men are waiting. And one of these days, surely, they will be surprised to find that they do not want to go back, they will dream of "a wonderful night, a wonderful lover, a white man." Possibly, too, they will become aware, one day, that "white men do not marry black women." But they have consented to run this risk; what they must have is whiteness at any price. For what reason? Nothing could be simpler. Here is a story that suits their minds:

> One day St. Peter saw three men arrive at the gate of heaven: a white man, a mulatto, and a Negro.
>
> "What do you want most?" he asked the white man.
>
> "Money."
>
> "And you?" he asked the mulatto.
>
> "Fame."
>
> St. Peter turned then to the Negro, who said with a wide smile:[7] "I'm just carrying these gentlemen's bags."

7. The smile of the black man, the *grin* [in English in the original], seems to have captured the interest of a number of writers. Here is what Bernard Wolfe says about it: "It pleases us to portray the Negro showing us all his teeth in a smile made for us. And his smile as we see it—as we make it—always means a *gift*. . . ."

Gifts without end, in every advertisement, on every screen, on every food-product label. . . . The black man gives Madame the new "dark Creole colors" for her pure nylons, courtesy of the House of Vigny; her "imaginative, coil-like" bottles of Golliwog toilet water and perfume. Shoeshines, clothes white as snow, comfortable lower berths, quick baggage-handling; jazz, jitterbug, jive, jokes, and the wonderful stories of Br'er Rabbit to amuse the little children. Service with a smile, every time. . . . "The blacks," writes anthropologist Geoffrey Gorer in *The American Spirit: A Study in National Char-*

Not long ago Etiemble described one of his disillusionments: "I was stupefied, as an adolescent, when a girl who knew me quite well jumped up in anger because I had said to her, in a situation where the word was not only appropriate but the one word that suited the occasion: 'You, as a Negress—.' 'Me? a Negress? Can't you see I'm practically white? I despise Negroes. Niggers stink. They're dirty and lazy. Don't ever mention niggers to me.' "[8]

I knew another black girl who kept a list of Parisian dance-halls "where-there-was-no-chance-of-running-into-niggers."

We must see whether it is possible for the black man to overcome his feeling of insignificance, to rid his life of the compulsive quality that makes it so like the behavior of the phobic. Affect is exacerbated in the Negro, he is full of rage because he feels small, he suffers from an inadequacy in all human communication, and all these factors chain him with an unbearable insularity.

Describing the phenomenon of ego-withdrawal, Anna Freud writes:

> As a method of avoiding "pain," ego-restriction, like the various forms of denial, does not come under the heading of the psychology of neurosis but is a normal stage in the development of the ego. When the ego is young and plastic, its withdrawal from one field of activity is sometimes com-

---

acter, "are kept in their obsequious attitude by the extreme penalties of fear and force, and this is common knowledge to both the whites and the blacks. Nevertheless, the whites demand that the blacks be always smiling, attentive, and friendly in all their relationships with them. . . ." ("L'oncle Rémus et son lapin," by Bernard Wolfe, *Les Temps Modernes,* May, 1949, p. 888.)

8. "Sur le *Martinique* de M. Michel Cournot," *Les Temps Modernes,* February, 1950.

> pensated for by excellence in another, upon which it concentrates. But, when it has become rigid or has already acquired an intolerance of "pain" and so is obsessionally fixated to a method of flight, such withdrawal is punished by impaired development. By abandoning one position after another it becomes one-sided, loses too many interests and can show but a meagre achievement.[9]

We understand now why the black man cannot take pleasure in his insularity. For him there is only one way out, and it leads into the white world. Whence his constant preoccupation with attracting the attention of the white man, his concern with being powerful like the white man, his determined effort to acquire protective qualities—that is, the proportion of being or having that enters into the composition of an ego. As I said earlier, it is from within that the Negro will seek admittance to the white sanctuary. The attitude derives from the intention.

Ego-withdrawal as a successful defense mechanism is impossible for the Negro. He requires a white approval.

In the midst of her mystical euphoria and her rhapsodic canticles, it seems to Mayotte Capécia that she is an angel and that she soars away "all pink and white." Nevertheless, in the film, *Green Pastures,* God and the angels are black, but the film was a brutal shock to our author: "How is it possible to imagine God with Negro characteristics? This is not my vision of paradise. But, after all, it was just an American film."[10]

Indeed no, the good and merciful God cannot be black: He is a white man with bright pink cheeks. From black to white is the course of mutation. One is white as one is

9. Anna Freud, *The Ego and the Mechanism of Defence* (New York, International Universities Press, 1946), p. 111.

10. Capécia, *op. cit.*, p. 65.

rich, as one is beautiful, as one is intelligent.

Meanwhile, André has departed to carry the *white message* to other Mayottes under other skies: delightful little genes with blue eyes, bicycling the whole length of the chromosome corridor. But, as a good white man, he has left instructions behind him. He is speaking of his and Mayotte's child: "You will bring him up, you will tell him about me, you will say, 'He was a superior person. You must work hard to be worthy of him.' "[11]

What about dignity? He had no need now to achieve it: It was injected now into the labyrinth of his arteries, entrenched in his little pink fingernails, a solidly rooted, white dignity.

And what about the father? This is what Etiemble has to say about him: "A fine specimen of his kind; he talked about the family, work, the nation, our good Pétain and our good God, all of which allowed him to make her pregnant according to form. God has made use of us, said the handsome swine, the handsome white man, the handsome officer. After which, under the same God-fearing Pétainist proprieties, I shove her over to the next man."

Before we have finished with her whose white lord is "like one dead" and who surrounds herself with dead men in a book crowded with deplorably dead things, we feel that we should like to ask Africa to send us a special envoy.[12]

---

11. *Ibid.*, p. 185.

12. After *Je suis Martiniquaise*, Mayotte Capécia wrote another book, *La négresse blanche*. She must have recognized her earlier mistakes, for in this book one sees an attempt to re-evaluate the Negro. But Mayotte Capécia did not reckon with her own unconscious. As soon as the novelist allows her characters a little freedom, they use it to belittle the Negro. All the Negroes whom she de-

Nor are we kept waiting. Abdoulaye Sadji, in *Nini*,[13] offers us a description of how black men can behave in contact with Europeans. I have said that Negrophobes exist. It is not hatred of the Negro, however, that motivates them; they lack the courage for that, or they have lost it. Hate is not inborn; it has to be constantly cultivated, to be brought into being, in conflict with more or less recognized guilt complexes. Hate demands existence, and he who hates has to show his hate in appropriate actions and behavior; in a sense, he has to become hate. That is why the Americans have substituted discrimination for lynching. Each to his own side of the street. Therefore we are not surprised that in the cities of (French?) black Africa there are European quarters. Mournier's work, *L'éveil de l'Afrique noire,* had already attracted my interest, but I was impatiently awaiting an African voice. Thanks to Alioune Diop's magazine, I have been able to coordinate the psychological motivations that govern men of color.

There is wonder, in the most religious sense of the word, in this passage:

---

scribes are in one way or another either semi-criminals or "sho' good" *niggers.*

In addition—and from this one can foresee what is to come—it is legitimate to say that Mayotte Capécia has definitively turned her back on her country. In both her books only one course is left for her heroines: to go away. This country of niggers is decidedly accursed. In fact, there is an aura of malediction surrounding Mayotte Capécia. But she is centrifugal. Mayotte Capécia is barred from herself.

May she add no more to the mass of her imbecilities.

Depart in peace, mudslinging storyteller. . . . But remember that, beyond your 500 anemic pages, it will always be possible to regain the honorable road that leads to the heart.

In spite of you.

13. In *Présence Africaine,* 1-2-3.

> M. Campian is the only white man in Saint-Louis who goes regularly to the Saint-Louis Club[14]—a man of a certain social standing, for he is an engineer with the Department of Bridges and Highways, as well as deputy director of Public Works in Senegal. He is said to be very much of a Negrophile, much more so than M. Roddin, who teaches at the Lycée Faidherbe and who gave a lecture on the equality of the races in the Saint-Louis Club itself. The good character of the one or the other is a constant theme for vehement discussions. In any event, M. Campian goes to the club more often, and there he has made the acquaintance of very well-behaved natives who show him much deference, who like him and who feel honored by his presence among them.[15]

The author, who is a teacher in black Africa, feels obligated to M. Roddin for his lecture on racial equality. I call this an outrage. One can understand the complaints that Mounier heard from the young Africans whom he had occasion to meet: "What we need here are Europeans like you." One is constantly aware that for the black man encountering a *toubab* with understanding offers a new hope of harmony.

Analyzing various passages of Abdoulaye Sadji's story, I shall attempt to grasp the living reactions of the woman of color to the European. First of all, there are two such women: the Negress and the mulatto. The first has only one possibility and one concern: to turn white. The second wants not only to turn white but also to avoid slipping back. What indeed could be more illogical than a mulatto woman's acceptance of a Negro husband? For it must be

14. A club frequented by the local young men. It stands across the street from the Civil Club, which is exclusively European.

15. Sadji, *op. cit.*, in *Présence Africaine*, no. 2, p. 280.

understood once and for all that it is a question of saving the race.

Hence Nini's great problem: A Negro has had the gall to go so far as to ask her to marry him. A Negro had the gall to write to her:

> The love that I offer you is pure and strong, it has nothing of a false tenderness intended to lull you with lies and illusions. . . . I want to see you happy, completely happy, in a setting to frame your qualities, which I believe I know how to appreciate. . . . I should consider it the highest of honors and the greatest of joys to have you in my house and to dedicate myself to you, body and soul. Your graces would illuminate my home and radiate light to the darkest corners. . . . Furthermore, I consider you too civilized and refined to reject brutally the offer of a devoted love concerned only with reassuring your happiness.[16]

This final sentence should not surprise us. Normally, the mulatto woman should refuse the presumptuous Negro without mercy. But, since she is civilized, she will not allow herself to see her lover's color, so that she can concentrate her attention on his devotion. Describing Mactar, Abdoulaye Sadji writes: "An idealist and a convinced advocate of unlimited progress, he still believed in the good faith of men, in their honesty, and he readily assumed that in everything merit alone must triumph."[17]

Who is Mactar? He has passed his baccalaureate, he is an accountant in the Department of Rivers, and he is pursuing a perfectly stupid little stenographer, who has, however, the least disputable quality: She is almost white. Therefore one must apologize for taking the liberty of

16. *Ibid.*, p. 286.
17. *Ibid.*, p. 281-282.

sending her a letter: "the utmost insolence, perhaps the first that any Negro had dared to attempt."[18]

One must apologize for daring to offer black love to a white soul. This we encounter again in René Maran: the fear, the timorousness, the humility of the black man in his relations with the white woman, or in any case with a woman whiter than he. Just as Mayotte Capécia tolerates anything from her lord, André, Mactar makes himself the slave of Nini, the mulatto. Prepared to sell his soul. But what is waiting for this boor is the law of plea in bar. The mulatto considers his letter an insult, an outrage to her honor as a "white lady." This Negro is an idiot, a scoundrel, an ignoramus who needs a lesson. That lesson she is prepared to give him; she will teach him to be more courteous and less brazen; she will make him understand that "white skins" are not for "*bougnouls*."[19]

Having learned the circumstances, the whole mulatto "society" plays chorus to her wrath. There is talk of taking the matter into court, of having the black man brought up on criminal charges. "There will be letters to the head of the Department of Public Works, to the governor of the colony, to call their attention to the black man's behavior and have him dismissed in recompense for the moral havoc that he has inflicted."[20]

Such an offense against principle should be punished by castration. And ultimately a request is made that Mactar

---

18. *Ibid.*, p. 281.

19. *Ibid.*, p. 287. *Bougnoul* is one of those untranslatable coinages of the rabble like the American *jigaboo*. Originated by the North African colonists, *bougnoul* means, generically, any "native" of a race *inferior* to that of the person using the word. (Translator's note.)

20. *Ibid.*, p. 288.

be formally reprimanded by the police. For, "if he returns to his unhealthy follies, we will have him brought into line by Police Inspector Dru, whose colleagues have nicknamed him the-real-bad-white-man."[21]

We have seen here how a girl of color reacts to a declaration of love made by one of her own. Let us inquire now what happens in the case of a white man. Once more we resort to Sadji. The long passage that he devotes to the reactions produced by the marriage of a white man and a mulatto will provide the vehicle.

> For some time a rumor had been repeated all over Saint-Louis. . . . It was at first a little whisper that went from one to another, making the wrinkled faces of the old "signaras" glow, putting new light into their dull eyes; then the younger women, showing the whites of their eyes and forming their heavy lips into circles, shouted the news, which caused amazement everywhere. "Oh, it can't be! . . . How do you know it's true? Can such things happen? . . . It's sweet. . . . It's such a scream." The news that had been running through Saint-Louis for a month was delightful, more delightful than all the promises in the world. It crowned a certain dream of grandeur, of distinction, which was common to all the mulatto women. The Ninis, the Nanas, and the Nénettes live wholly outside the natural conditions of their country. The great dream that haunts every one of them is to be the bride of a white man from Europe. One could say that all their efforts are directed to this end, which is almost never attained. Their need to gesticulate, their love of ridiculous ostentation, their calculated, theatrical, revolting attitudes, are just so many effects of the same mania for grandeur. They must have white men, completely white, and nothing else will do. Almost all of them spend their entire lives waiting for this stroke of luck, which is anything but likely. And they are still waiting when old age

21. *Ibid.*, p. 289.

> overtakes them and forces them deep into dark refuges where the dream finally grows into a haughty resignation. . . .
>
> Very delightful news. . . . M. Darrivey, a completely white European employed in the civil service, had formally requested the hand of Dédée, a mulatto who was only half-Negro. It was unbelievable.[22]

Something remarkable must have happened on the day when the white man declared his love to the mulatto. There was recognition, incorporation into a group that had seemed hermetic. The psychological minus-value, this feeling of insignificance and its corollary, the impossibility of reaching the light, totally vanished. From one day to the next, the mulatto went from the class of slaves to that of masters.

She had been recognized through her overcompensating behavior. She was no longer the woman who wanted to be white; she was white. She was joining the white world.

In *Magic noire*, Paul Morand described a similar phenomenon, but one has since learned to be leery of Paul Morand. From the psychological point of view, it may be interesting to consider the following problem. The educated mulatto woman, especially if she is a student, engages in doubly equivocal behavior. She says, "I do not like the Negro because he is savage. Not savage in a cannibal way, but lacking refinement." An abstract point of view. And when one points out to her that in this respect some black people may be her superiors, she falls back on their "ugliness." A factitious point of view. Faced with the proofs of a genuine black esthetic, she

22. *Ibid.*, p. 489.

professes to be unable to understand it; one tries then to explain its canon to her; the wings of her nose flare, there is a sharp intake of breath, "she is free to choose her own husband." As a last resort, the appeal to subjectivity. If, as Anna Freud says, the ego is driven to desperation by the amputation of all its defense mechanisms, "in so far as the bringing of the unconscious activities of the ego into consciousness has the effect of disclosing the defensive processes and rendering them inoperative, the result of analysis is to weaken the ego still further and to advance the pathological process."[23]

But in Dédée's case the ego does not have to defend itself, since its claims have been officially recognized: She is marrying a white man. Every coin, however, has two sides; whole families have been made fools of. Three or four mulatto girls had acquired mulatto admirers, while all their friends had white men. "This was looked on particularly as an insult to the family as a whole; an offense, moreover, that required amends."[24] For these families had been humiliated in their most legitimate ambitions; the mutilation that they had suffered affected the very movement of their lives, the rhythm of their existence. . . .

In response to a profound desire they sought to change, to "evolve." This right was denied to them. At any rate, it was challenged.

What is there to say, after these expositions?

Whether one is dealing with Mayotte Capécia of Martinique or with Nini of Saint-Louis, the same process is to be observed. A bilateral process, an attempt to acquire—by internalizing them—assets that were originally prohib-

23. Anna Freud, *op. cit.*, p. 70.
24. Sadji, *op. cit.*, p. 498.

ited. It is because the Negress feels inferior that she aspires to win admittance into the white world. In this endeavor she will seek the help of a phenomenon that we shall call *affective erethism.*

This work represents the sum of the experiences and observations of seven years; regardless of the area I have studied, one thing has struck me: The Negro enslaved by his inferiority, the white man enslaved by his superiority alike behave in accordance with a neurotic orientation. Therefore I have been led to consider their alienation in terms of psychoanalytical classifications. The Negro's behavior makes him akin to an obsessive neurotic type, or, if one prefers, he puts himself into a complete situational neurosis. In the man of color there is a constant effort to run away from his own individuality, to annihilate his own presence. Whenever a man of color protests, there is alienation. Whenever a man of color rebukes, there is alienation. We shall see later, in Chapter Six, that the Negro, having been made inferior, proceeds from humiliating insecurity through strongly voiced self-accusation to despair. The attitude of the black man toward the white, or toward his own race, often duplicates almost completely a constellation of delirium, frequently bordering on the region of the pathological.

It will be objected that there is nothing psychotic in the Negroes who are discussed here. Nevertheless I should like to cite two highly significant instances. A few years ago I knew a Negro medical student. He had an *agonizing* conviction that he was not taken at his true worth—not on the university level, he explained, but as a human being. He had an *agonizing* conviction that he would never succeed in gaining recognition as a colleague from the whites in his profession and as a physician from his

European patients. In such moments of fantasy intuition,[25] the times most favorable[26] to psychosis, he would get drunk. Finally, he enlisted one day in the army as a medical officer; and, he added, not for anything in the world would he agree to go to the colonies or to serve in a colonial unit. He wanted to have white men under his command. He was a boss; as such he was to be feared or respected. That was just what he wanted, what he strove for: to make white men adopt a Negro attitude toward him. In this way he was obtaining revenge for the *imago* that had always obsessed him: the frightened, trembling Negro, abased before the white overlord.

I had another acquaintance, a customs inspector in a port on the French mainland, who was extremely severe with tourists or travelers in transit. "Because," he explained to me, "if you aren't a bastard they take you for a poor shit. Since I'm a Negro, you can imagine how I'm going to get it either way. . . ."

In *Understanding Human Nature*, Adler says:

> When we demonstrate cases . . . it is frequently convenient to show relationships between the childhood impressions and the actual complaint . . . this is best done by a graph. . . . We will succeed in many cases in being able to plot this graph of life, the spiritual curve along which the entire movement of an individual has taken place. The equation of the curve is the behavior pattern which this individual has followed since earliest childhood. . . . Actually we see this behavior pattern, whose final configuration is subject to some few changes, but whose essential content, whose energy and meaning remain unchanged from earliest childhood, is the determining factor, even though the relations

25. Dublineau, *L'intuition délirante*.
26. Jacques Lacan.

to the adult environment . . . may tend to modify it in some instances.[27]

We are anticipating, and it is already clear that the individual psychology of Adler will help us to understand the conception of the world held by the man of color. Since the black man is a former slave, we will turn to Hegel too; and, to conclude, Freud should be able to contribute to our study.

Nini and Mayotte Capécia: two types of behavior that move us to thought.

Are there no other possibilities?

But those are pseudo-questions that do not concern us. I will say, however, that every criticism of that which is implies a solution, if indeed one can propose a solution to one's fellow—to a free being.

What I insist on is that the poison must be eliminated once and for all.

27. Alfred Adler, *Understanding Human Nature* (New York, Greenberg, 1927), p. 80.

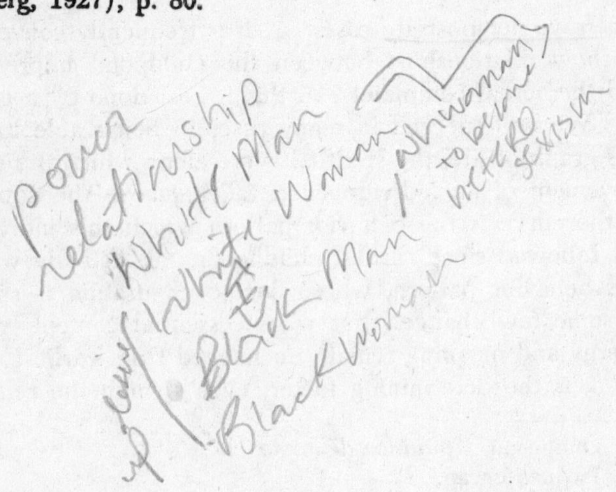

Chapter Three

THE MAN OF COLOR AND THE WHITE WOMAN

Out of the blackest part of my soul, across the zebra striping of my mind, surges this desire to be suddenly *white.*

I wish to be acknowledged not as *black* but as *white.*

Now—and this is a form of recognition that Hegel had not envisaged—who but a white woman can do this for me? By loving me she proves that I am worthy of white love. I am loved like a white man.

I am a white man.

Her love takes me onto the noble road that leads to total realization. . . .

I marry white culture, white beauty, white whiteness.

When my restless hands caress those white breasts, they grasp white civilization and dignity and make them mine.

Some thirty years ago, a coal-black Negro, in a Paris bed with a "maddening" blonde, shouted at the moment of orgasm, "Hurrah for Schoelcher!" When one recalls that it was Victor Schoelcher who persuaded the Third Republic to adopt the decree abolishing slavery, one understands why it is necessary to elaborate somewhat on the possible aspects of relations between black men and white women.

It will be argued that this little tale is not authenticated; but simply that it could be born and survive through the years is an indication: It is no fallacy. For the anecdote renews a conflict that, active or dormant, is always real. Its persistence attests to the black world's endorsement. To say it another way, when a story flourishes in the heart of a folklore, it is because in one way or another it expresses an aspect of "the spirit of the group."

In analyzing *Je suis Martiniquaise* and *Nini*, we have seen how the Negress behaves with the white man. Through a novel by René Maran—which seems to be autobiographical—let us try to understand what happens when the man is black and the woman white.

The problem is admirably laid out, for the character of Jean Veneuse will make it possible for us to go much more deeply into the attitude of the black man. What are the terms of this problem? Jean Veneuse is a Negro. Born in the Antilles, he has lived in Bordeaux for years; so he is a European. But he is black; so he is a Negro. There is the conflict. He does not understand his own race, and the whites do not understand him. And, he observes, "The Europeans in general and the French in particular, not satisfied with simply ignoring the Negro of the colonies, repudiate the one whom they have shaped into their own image."[1]

The personality of the author does not emerge quite so easily as one might wish. An orphan sent to a provincial boarding-school, he is compelled to spend his vacations there. His friends and acquaintances scatter all over France on the slightest pretext, whereas the little Negro

1. *Un homme pareil aux autres* (Paris, Editions Arc-en-Ciel, 1947), p. 11.

is forced into the habit of solitude, so that his best friends are his books. At the extreme, I should say there is a certain accusatory character, a certain resentment, an ill-disciplined aggression, in the long list—too long—of "traveling companions" that the author offers us: at the extreme, I say, but it is exactly to the extreme that we have to go.

Unable to be assimilated, unable to pass unnoticed, he consoles himself by associating with the dead, or at least the absent. And his associations, unlike his life, ignore the barriers of centuries and oceans. He talks with Marcus Aurelius, Joinville, Pascal, Pérez Galdós, Rabindranath Tagore. If we were compelled to hang a label on Jean Veneuse, we should have to call him an introvert; others might call him a sentimentalist, but a sentimentalist who is always careful to contrive a way of winning out on the level of ideas and knowledge. As a matter of fact, his friends and schoolmates hold him in high regard: "What a perpetual dreamer! You know, my old pal, Veneuse, is really a character. He never takes his nose out of his books except to scribble all over his notebooks."[2]

But a sentimentalist who goes nonstop from singing Spanish songs to translating into English. Shy, but uneasy as well: "As I was leaving them, I heard Divrande say to him: 'A good kid, that Veneuse—he seems to like being sad and quiet, but he's always helpful. You can trust him. You'll see. He's the kind of Negro that a lot of white guys ought to be like.'"[3]

Uneasy and anxious indeed. An anxious man who cannot escape his body. We know from other sources that René Maran cherished an affection for André Gide. It

2. *Ibid.*, p. 87.
3. *Ibid.*, pp. 18-19.

seems possible to find a resemblance between the ending of *Un homme pareil aux autres* and that of Gide's *Strait is the Gate*. This departure, this tone of emotional pain, of moral impossibility, seems an echo of the story of Jérôme and Alissa.

But there remains the fact that Veneuse is black. He is a bear who loves solitude. He is a thinker. And when a woman tries to start a flirtation with him, he says, "Are you trying to smoke out an old bear like me? Be careful, my dear. Courage is a fine thing, but you're going to get yourself talked about if you go on attracting attention this way. A Negro? Shameful—it's beneath contempt. Associating with anybody of that race is just utterly disgracing yourself."[4]

Above all, he wants to prove to the others that he is a man, their equal. But let us not be misled: Jean Veneuse is the man who has to be convinced. It is in the roots of his soul, as complicated as that of any European, that the doubt persists. If the expression may be allowed, Jean Veneuse is the lamb to be slaughtered. Let us make the effort.

After having quoted Stendhal and mentioned the phenomenon of "crystallization," he declares that he loves

> Andrée spiritually in Mme. Coulanges and physically in Clarisse. It is insane. But that is how it is: I love Clarisse, I love Mme. Coulanges, even though I never really think of either of them. All they are for me is an excuse that makes it possible for me to delude myself. I study Andrée in them and I begin to know her by heart. . . . I don't know. I know nothing. I have no wish to try to know anything; or, rather, I know nothing any more except one thing: that the Negro is a man like the rest, the equal of the others, and that his heart, which only the ignorant consider simple,

4. *Ibid.*, pp. 45-46.

can be as complicated as the heart of the most complicated of Europeans.[5]

For the simplicity of the Negro is a myth created by superficial observers. "I love Clarisse, I love Mme. Coulanges, and it is Andrée Marielle whom I really love. Only she, no one else."[6]

Who is Andrée Marielle? You know who she is, the daughter of the poet, Louis Marielle. But now you see that this Negro, "who has raised himself through his own intelligence and his assiduous labors to the level of the thought and the culture of Europe,"[7] is incapable of escaping his race.

Andrée Marielle is white; no solution seems possible. Yet, association with Payot, Gide, Moréas, and Voltaire seemed to have wiped out all that. In all good faith, Jean Veneuse "believed in that culture and set himself to love this new world he had discovered and conquered for his own use. What a blunder he had made! Arriving at maturity and going off to serve his adopted country in the land of his ancestors was enough to make him wonder whether he was not being betrayed by everything about him, for the white race would not accept him as one of its own and the black virtually repudiated him."[8]

Jean Veneuse, feeling that existence is impossible for him without love, proceeds to dream it into being. He proceeds to dream it alive and to produce verses:

> When a man loves he must not speak;
> Best that he hide it from himself.

---

5. *Ibid.*, p. 83.
6. *Ibid.*, p. 83.
7. *Ibid.*, p. 36.
8. *Ibid.*, p. 36.

Andrée Marielle has written to him that she loves him, but Jean Veneuse needs authorization. It is essential that some white man say to him, "Take my sister." Veneuse has put a certain number of questions to his friend, Coulanges. Here, more or less *in extenso,* is what Coulanges answers:

> Old boy [Coulanges uses the English expression],
>
> Once again you bring me your problem, once again I will give you my opinion—once and for all. Let us proceed in an orderly fashion. Your situation as you have explained it to me is as clear as it can be. Allow me nevertheless to clear the ground before me. It will be all to your good.
>
> How old were you, anyway, when you left home to go to France? Three or four, I think. You have never seen your native island since, and you have not the slightest interest in seeing it again. You have lived in Bordeaux ever since. And ever since you became a colonial official, Bordeaux is where you have spent the greatest part of your leaves. In short, you are really one of us. Perhaps you are not altogether aware of the fact. In that case, accept the fact that you are a Frenchman from Bordeaux. Get that into your thick head. You know nothing of your compatriots of the Antilles. I should be amazed, in fact, if you could even manage to communicate with them. The ones I know, furthermore, have no resemblance to you.
>
> In fact you are like us—you are "us." Your thoughts are ours. You behave as we behave, as we would behave. You think of yourself—others think of you—as a Negro? Utterly mistaken! You merely look like one. As for everything else, you think as a European. And so it is natural that you love as a European. Since European men love only European women, you can hardly marry anyone but a woman of the country where you have always lived, a woman of our good old France, your real and only country. This being the case, let us get on to the subject of your latest letter. On the one hand we have one Jean Veneuse, who resembles you like a

> brother; on the other hand we have Mlle. Andrée Marielle. Andrée Marielle, whose skin is white, loves Jean Veneuse, who is extremely brown and who adores Andrée Marielle. But that does not stop you from asking me what must be done. You magnificent idiot! . . .
>
> As soon as you are back in France, rush to the father of the girl who already belongs to you in spirit and strike your fist savagely on your heart as you shout at him: "I love her. She loves me. We love each other. She must marry me. Otherwise I will kill myself here and now."[9]

When the question is put directly, then, the white man agrees to give his sister to the black—but on one condition: You have nothing in common with real Negroes. You are not black, you are "extremely brown."

This procedure is quite familiar to colored students in France. Society refuses to consider them genuine Negroes. The Negro is a savage, whereas the student is civilized. "You're 'us,'" Coulanges tells him; and if anyone thinks you are a Negro he is mistaken, because you merely look like one. But Jean Veneuse does not want this. He cannot accept it, because he knows.

He knows that, "enraged by this degrading ostracism, mulattoes and Negroes have only one thought from the moment they land in Europe: to gratify their appetite for white women."

> The majority of them, including those of lighter skin who often go to the extreme of denying both their countries and their mothers, tend to marry in Europe not so much out of love as for the satisfaction of being the master of a European woman; and a certain tang of proud revenge enters into this.
>
> And so I wonder whether in my case there is any difference from theirs; whether, by marrying you, who are a

9. *Ibid.*, pp. 152-154.

> European, I may not appear to be making a show of contempt for the women of my own race and, above all, to be drawn on by desire for that white flesh that has been forbidden to us Negroes as long as white men have ruled the world, so that without my knowledge I am attempting to revenge myself on a European woman for everything that her ancestors have inflicted on mine throughout the centuries.[10]

What a struggle to free himself of a purely subjective conflict. I am a white man, I was born in Europe, all my friends are white. There are not eight Negroes in the city where I live. I think in French, France is my religion. I am a European, do you understand? I am not a Negro, and in order to prove it to you, I as a public employe am going to show the genuine Negroes the differences that separate me from them. Indeed, read the book again and you will be convinced:

> Who knocked at the door? Ah, yes, of course.
> "Is that you, Soua?"
> "Yes, major."
> "What do you want?"
> "Roll call, major. Five men guard. Seventeen men prisoners—everybody here."
> "Anything else new? Any word from the runner?"
> "No, suh, major."[11]

Monsieur Veneuse has native bearers. He has a young Negro girl in his house. And to the Negroes who seem downcast that he is leaving, he feels that the only thing for him to say is, "Please go away. Please go away. You see . . . how unhappy it makes me to leave you. Please go

10. *Ibid.*, p. 185.
11. *Ibid.*, p. 162.

now. I will not forget you. I am leaving you only because this is not my country and I feel too alone here, too empty, too deprived of all the comfort that I need but that you, luckily for you, do not yet require."[12]

When we read such passages we cannot help thinking of Félix Eboué, unquestionably a Negro, who saw his duty quite differently in the same circumstances. Jean Veneuse is not a Negro and does not wish to be a Negro. And yet, without his knowledge, a gulf has been created. There is something indefinable, irreversible, there is indeed the *that within* of Harold Rosenberg.[13]

Louis-T. Achille said in his report to the Interracial Conferences of 1949:

> Insofar as truly interracial marriage is concerned, one can legitimately wonder to what extent it may not represent for the colored spouse a kind of subjective consecration to wiping out in himself and in his own mind the color prejudice from which he has suffered so long. It would be interesting to investigate this in a given number of cases and perhaps to seek in this clouded motivation the underlying reason for certain interracial marriages entered into outside the normal conditions of a happy household. Some men or some women, in effect, by choosing partners of another race, marry persons of a class or a culture inferior to their own whom they would not have chosen as spouses in their own race and whose chief asset seems to be the assurance that the partner will achieve denaturalization and (to use a loathsome word) "deracialization." Among certain people of color, the fact that they are marrying someone of the white race seems to have overridden every other considera-

---

12. *Ibid.*, p. 213.

13. "Du Jeu au Je, Esquisse d'une géographie de l'action," *Les Temps Modernes*, April, 1948, p. 1732.

> tion. In this fact they find access to complete equality with that illustrious race, the master of the world, the ruler of the peoples of color. . . .[14]

We know historically that the Negro guilty of lying with a white woman is castrated. The Negro who has had a white woman makes himself taboo to his fellows. It is easy for the mind to formulate this drama of sexual preoccupation. And that is exactly the ultimate goal of the archetype of *Uncle Remus:* Br'er Rabbit, who represents the black man. Will he or will he not succeed in going to bed with the two daughters of Mrs. Meadows? There are ups and downs, all told by a laughing, good-natured, easygoing Negro, a Negro who serves with a smile.

During the time when I was slowly being jolted alive into puberty, I had the honor of being able to look in wonder on one of my older friends who had just come back from France and who had held a Parisian girl in his arms. I shall try to analyze this problem in a special chapter.

Talking recently with several Antilleans, I found that the dominant concern among those arriving in France was to go to bed with a white woman. As soon as their ships docked in Le Havre, they were off to the houses. Once this ritual of initiation into "authentic" manhood had been fulfilled, they took the train for Paris.

But what is important here is to examine Jean Veneuse. To this end, I shall resort in considerable measure to a study by Germaine Guex, *La névrose d'abandon.*

Contrasting what she calls the abandonment neurosis, which is pre-Oedipal in nature, to the real post-Oedipal conflicts described by orthodox Freudians, Dr. Guex ana-

14. *Rythmes du Monde,* 1949, p. 113.

lyzes two types, the first of which seems to illustrate the plight of Jean Veneuse: "It is this tripod—the *anguish* created by every abandonment, the *aggression* to which it gives rise, and the *devaluation of self* that flows out of it—that supports the whole symptomatology of this neurosis."[15]

We made an introvert of Jean Veneuse. We know characterologically—or, better, phenomenologically—that autistic thinking can be made dependent on a primary introversion.[16]

> In a patient of the negative-aggressive type, obsession with the past and with its frustrations, its gaps, its defeats, paralyzes his enthusiasm for living. Generally more introverted than the positive-loving type, he has a tendency to go back over his past and present disappointments, building up in himself a more or less secret area of bitter, disillusioned resentments that often amounts to a kind of autism. But, unlike the genuine autistic person, the abandonment-neurotic is aware of this secret zone, which he cultivates and defends against every intrusion. More egocentric than the neurotic of the second type (positive-loving), he views everything in terms of himself. He has little capacity for disinterestedness: His aggressions and a constant need for vengeance inhibit his impulses. His retreat into himself does not allow him to have any positive experience that would compensate for his past. Hence the lack of self-esteem and therefore of affective security is virtually total in such cases; and as a result there is an overwhelming feeling of impotence in relation to life and to people, as well as a complete rejection of the feeling of responsibility. Others have betrayed him and thwarted him, and yet it is only

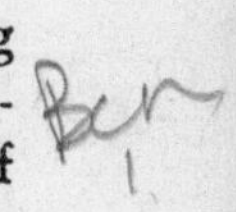

15. G. Guex, *La Névrose d'abandon* (Paris, Presses Universitaires de France, 1950), p. 13.

16. E. Minkowski, *La Schizophrénie* (Paris, Payot, 1927).

from these others that he expects any improvement in his lot.[17]

A magnificent description, into which the character of Jean Veneuse fits perfectly. For, he tells us, "arriving at maturity and going off to serve my adopted country in the land of my ancestors was enough to make me wonder *whether I was not being betrayed*[18] by everything about me, for the white race would not accept me as one of its own and the black virtually repudiated me. That is precisely my position."[19]

The attitude is one of recrimination toward the past, devaluation of self, incapability of being understood as he would like to be. Listen again to Jean Veneuse:

> Who can describe the desperation of the little *Hottentots* whose parents, in the hope of making real Frenchmen of them, transplant them to France too early? From one day to the next they are locked into boarding schools, these free, joyful children, "for your own good," as their weeping parents tell them.
>
> I was one of these intermittent orphans, and I shall suffer for it throughout my life. At the age of seven I and my introduction to learning were turned over to a gloomy school far out in the country. . . . The thousand games that are supposed to enliven childhood and adolescence could not make me forget how painful mine were. It is to this schooling that my character owes its inner melancholy and that fear of social contact that today inhibits even my slightest impulses. . . .[20]

And yet he would have liked to be surrounded, enclosed. He did not like to be *abandoned*. When school

17. Guex, *op. cit.*, pp. 27-28.
18. My italics—F.F.
19. Maran, *op. cit.*, p. 36.
20. *Ibid.*, p. 227.

vacations came, all the other boys went home; alone—note that word *alone*—he remained in the big empty white school. . . .

> Oh, those tears of a child who had no one to wipe them. . . . He will never forget that he was apprenticed so young to loneliness. . . . A cloistered existence, a withdrawn, secluded existence in which I learned too soon to meditate and to reflect. A solitary life that in the end was profoundly moved by trifles—it has made me hypersensitive within myself, incapable of externalizing my joys or my sorrows, so that I reject everything that I love and I turn my back in spite of myself on everything that attracts me.[21]

What is going on here? Two processes. I do not want to be loved. Why not? Because once, very long ago, I attempted an object relation and I was *abandoned*. I have never forgiven my mother. Because I was abandoned, I will make someone else suffer, and desertion by me will be the direct expression of my need for revenge. I will go to Africa: I do not wish to be loved and I will flee from love-objects. That, Germaine Guex says, is called "putting oneself to the proof in order to prove something." I do not wish to be loved, I adopt a defensive position. And if the love-object insists, I will say plainly, "I do not wish to be loved."

Devaluation of self? Indeed yes.

> This lack of esteem of self as an object worthy of love has grave consequences. For one thing, it keeps the individual in a state of profound inner insecurity, as a result of which it inhibits or falsifies every relation with others. It is as something that has the right to arouse sympathy or love that the individual is uncertain of himself. The lack of affective self-valuation is to be found only in persons who

---

21. *Ibid.*, p. 228.

in their early childhood suffered from a lack of love and understanding.[22]

Jean Veneuse would like to be a man like the rest, but he knows that this position is a false one. He is a beggar. He looks for appeasement, for permission in the white man's eyes. For to him there is "The Other."

> Affective self-rejection invariably brings the abandonment-neurotic to an extremely painful and obsessive feeling of exclusion, of having no place anywhere, of being superfluous everywhere in an affective sense. . . . "I am The Other" is an expression that I have heard time and again in the language of the abandonment-neurotic. To be "The Other" is to feel that one is always in a shaky position, to be always on guard, ready to be rejected and . . . unconsciously doing everything needed to bring about exactly this catastrophe.
>
> It would be impossible to overestimate the intensity of the suffering that accompanies such desertion states, a suffering that in one way is connected to the first experiences of rejection in childhood and that brings them back in all their strength. . . .[23]

The abandonment-neurotic demands proofs. He is not satisfied with isolated statements. He has no confidence. Before he forms an objective relation, he exacts repeated proofs from his partner. The essence of his attitude is "not to love in order to avoid being abandoned." The abandonment-neurotic is insatiable. That is because he claims the right to constant amends. He wants to be loved completely, absolutely and forever. Listen:

> My dearest Jean,
>
> I got your letter of last July only today. It is completely

22. Guex, *op. cit.*, pp. 31-32.
23. *Ibid.*, pp. 35-36.

mad. Why torture me this way? You—are you aware of the fact?—you are incomparably cruel. You give me happiness mixed with anxiety. You make me the happiest and at the same time the unhappiest of women. How many times shall I have to tell you that I love you, that I belong to you, that I am waiting for you? Come.[24]

The abandonment-neurotic has finally deserted. He is called back. He is needed. He is loved. And yet what fantasies! Does she really love me? Does she look at me objectively?

"One day a man came, a great friend of Daddy Ned who had never seen Pontaponte. He came from Bordeaux. But good God, he was dirty! God, how ugly he was, this man who was such a good friend of Daddy Ned! He had a hideous black face, completely black, which showed that he must not wash very often."[25]

Looking eagerly for external reasons for his Cinderella complex, Jean Veneuse projects the entire arsenal of racial stereotypes onto a child of three or four years. And to Andrée he says, "Tell me, Andrée darling . . . in spite of my color, would you agree to marry me if I asked you?"[26]

He is frightfully full of doubt. Here is Germaine Guex on that subject:

> The first characteristic seems to be the dread of showing oneself as one actually is. This is a broad field of various fears: fear of disappointing, fear of displeasing, of boring, of wearying . . . and consequently of losing the chance to create a bond of sympathy with others or if this bond does exist of doing damage to it. The abandonment-neurotic doubts whether he can be loved as he is, for he has had the cruel experience of being abandoned when he offered

24. Maran, *op. cit.*, pp. 203-204.
25. *Ibid.*, pp. 84-85.
26. *Ibid.*, pp. 247-248.

himself to the tenderness of others as a little child and hence without artifice.[27]

Jean Veneuse does not, however, lead a life devoid of compensations. He flirts with art. His reading list is impressive, his essay on Suarès is quite perceptive. That too is analyzed by Germaine Guex: "Imprisoned in himself, locked into his artificial reserve, the negative-aggressive feeds his feeling of irreparable loss with everything that he continues to lose or that his passivity makes him lack. . . . Therefore, with the exception of such privileged sectors as *his intellectual life or his profession*,[28] he cherishes a deep-seated feeling of worthlessness."[29]

Where does this analysis lead us? To nothing short of proving to Jean Veneuse that in fact he is not like the rest. Making people ashamed of their existence, Jean-Paul Sartre said. Yes: teaching them to become aware of the potentials they have forbidden themselves, of the passivity they have paraded in just those situations in which what is needed is to hold oneself, like a sliver, to the heart of the world, to interrupt if necessary the rhythm of the world, to upset, if necessary, the chain of command, but in any case, and most assuredly, *to stand up to the world.*

Jean Veneuse is the crusader of the inner life. When he sees Andrée again, when he is face to face with this woman whom he has wanted for months and months, he takes refuge in silence, the eloquent silence of those who "know the artificiality of words and acts."

Jean Veneuse is a neurotic, and his color is only an attempt to explain his psychic structure. If this objective

---

27. Guex, *op. cit.*, p. 39.
28. My italics—F.F.
29. Guex, *op. cit.*, p. 44.

difference had not existed, he would have manufactured it out of nothing.

Jean Veneuse is one of those intellectuals who try to take a position solely on the level of ideas. Incapable of realizing any concrete contact with his fellow man. Is he treated decently, kindly, humanly? Only because he has stumbled on some servant secrets. He "knows those people," and he is on guard against them. "My vigilance, if one can call it that, is a safety-catch. Politely and artlessly I welcome the advances that are made to me. I accept and repay the drinks that are bought for me, I take part in the little social games that are played on deck, but I do not allow myself to be taken in by the good will shown me, suspicious as I am of this excessive cordiality that has rather too quickly taken the place of the hostility in the midst of which they formerly tried to isolate me."[30]

He accepts the drinks, but he buys others in return. He does not wish to be obligated to anyone. For if he does not buy back, he is a nigger, as ungrateful as all the others.

Is someone mean? It is simply because he is a nigger. For it is impossible not to despise him. Well, it is clear to me that Jean Veneuse, alias René Maran, is neither more nor less than a black abandonment-neurotic. And he is put back into his place, his proper place. He is a neurotic who needs to be emancipated from his infantile fantasies. And I contend that Jean Veneuse represents not an example of black-white relations, but a certain mode of behavior in a neurotic who by coincidence is black. So the purpose of our study becomes more precise: to enable the man of color to understand, through specific examples, the psychological elements that can alienate his fellow Negroes.

30. Maran, *op. cit.*, p. 103.

I will emphasize this further in the chapter devoted to phenomenological description, but let us remember that our purpose is to make possible a healthy encounter between black and white.

Jean Veneuse is ugly. He is black. What more is needed? If one rereads the various observations of Germaine Guex, one will be convinced by the evidence: *Un homme pareil aux autres* is a sham, an attempt to make the relations between two races dependent on an organic unhealthiness. There can be no argument: In the domain of psychoanalysis as in that of philosophy, the organic, or constitutional, is a myth only for him who can go beyond it. If from a heuristic point of view one must totally deny the existence of the organic, the fact remains, and we can do nothing about it, that some individuals make every effort to fit into pre-established categories. Or, rather, yes, we can do something about it.

Earlier I referred to Jacques Lacan; it was not by accident. In his thesis, presented in 1932, he violently attacked the idea of the constitutional. Apparently I am departing from his conclusions, but my dissent will be understood when one recalls that for the idea of the constitutional as it is understood by the French school I am substituting that of structure—"embracing unconscious psychic life, as we are able to know it in part, especially in the form of repression and inhibition, insofar as these elements take an active part in the organization peculiar to each psychic individuality." [31]

As we have seen, on examination Jean Veneuse displays the structure of an abandonment-neurotic of the negative-aggressive type. One can attempt to explain this

31. Guex, *op. cit.*, p. 54.

reactionally—that is, through the interaction of person and environment—and prescribe, for example, a new environment, "a change of air." It will properly be observed that in this case the structure has remained constant. The change of air that Jean Veneuse prescribed for himself was not undertaken in order to find himself as a man; he did not have as his purpose the formulation of a healthy outlook on the world; he had no striving toward the productiveness that is characteristic of psychosocial equilibrium, but sought rather to corroborate his *externalizing* neurosis.

The neurotic structure of an individual is simply the elaboration, the formation, the eruption within the ego, of conflictual clusters arising in part out of the environment and in part out of the purely personal way in which that individual reacts to these influences.

Just as there was a touch of fraud in trying to deduce from the behavior of Nini and Mayotte Capécia a general law of the behavior of the black woman with the white man, there would be a similar lack of objectivity, I believe, in trying to extend the attitude of Veneuse to the man of color as such. And I should like to think that I have discouraged any endeavors to connect the defeats of Jean Veneuse with the greater or lesser concentration of melanin in his epidermis.

This sexual myth—the quest for white flesh—perpetuated by alienated psyches, must no longer be allowed to impede active understanding.

In no way should my color be regarded as a flaw. From the moment the Negro accepts the separation imposed by the European he has no further respite, and "is it not understandable that thenceforward he will try to elevate himself to the white man's level? To elevate himself in the range of colors to which he attributes a kind of hierarchy?"[32]

We shall see that another solution is possible. It implies a restructuring of the world.

32. Claude Nordey, *L'homme de couleur* (Paris, Collection "Présences," Plon, 1939).

Chapter Four

THE SO-CALLED DEPENDENCY COMPLEX OF COLONIZED PEOPLES

> *In the whole world no poor devil is lynched, no wretch is tortured, in whom I too am not degraded and murdered.*
>
> —*Aimé Césaire,* Et les chiens se taisent

When I embarked on this study, only a few essays by Mannoni, published in a magazine called *Psyché,* were available to me. I was thinking of writing to M. Mannoni to ask about the conclusions to which his investigations had led him. Later I learned that he had gathered his reflections in a forthcoming book. It has now been published: *Prospero and Caliban: Psychology of Colonization.* Let us examine it.

Before going into details, I should like to say that its analytic thought is honest. Having lived under the extreme ambivalence inherent in the colonial situation, M. Mannoni has managed to achieve a grasp—unfortunately too exhaustive—of the psychological phenomena that govern the relations between the colonized and the colonizer.

The basic characteristic of current psychological research seems to be the achievement of a certain exhaustiveness. But one should not lose sight of the real.

I propose to show that, although he has devoted 225 pages to the study of the colonial situation, M. Mannoni has not understood its real coordinates.

When one approaches a problem as important as that of taking inventory of the possibilities for understanding between two different peoples, one should be doubly careful.

Mr. Mannoni deserves our thanks for having introduced into the procedure two elements whose importance can never again escape anyone.

A quick analysis had seemed to avoid subjectivity in this field. M. Mannoni's study is sincere in purpose, for it proposes to prove the impossibility of explaining man outside the limits of his capacity for accepting or denying a given situation. Thus the problem of colonialism includes not only the interrelations of objective historical conditions but also human attitudes toward these conditions.

Similarly, I can subscribe to that part of M. Mannoni's work that tends to present the pathology of the conflict—that is, to show that the white colonial is motivated only by his desire to put an end to a feeling of unsatisfaction, on the level of Adlerian overcompensation.

At the same time, I find myself opposing him when I read a sentence like this: "The fact that when an *adult* Malagasy is isolated in a different environment he can become susceptible to the classical type of inferiority complex proves almost beyond doubt that the germ of the complex was latent in him from childhood."[1]

In reading this one feels something turn upside down, and the author's "objectivity" threatens to lead one into error.

Nevertheless, I have tried zealously to retrace his line

1. [Dominique] O. Mannoni, *Prospero and Caliban: The Psychology of Colonization* (New York, Praeger, 1964), p. 40.

of orientation, the fundamental theme of his book: "The central idea is that the confrontation of 'civilized' and 'primitive' men creates a special situation—the colonial situation—and brings about the *emergence* of a mass of illusions and misunderstandings that only a psychological analysis can place and define."[2]

Now, since this is M. Mannoni's point of departure, why does he try to make the inferiority complex something that antedates colonization? Here one perceives the mechanism of explanation that, in psychiatry, would give us this: There are latent forms of psychosis that become overt as the result of a traumatic experience. Or, in somatic medicine, this: The appearance of varicose veins in a patient does not arise out of his being compelled to spend ten hours a day on his feet, but rather out of the constitutional weakness of his vein walls; his working conditions are only a complicating factor. And the insurance compensation expert to whom the case is submitted will find the responsibility of the employer extremely limited.

Before taking up M. Mannoni's conclusions in detail, I should like to make my position clear. Once and for all I will state this principle: A given society is racist or it is not. Until all the evidence is available, a great number of problems will have to be put aside. Statements, for example, that the north of France is more racist than the south, that racism is the work of underlings and hence in no way involves the ruling class, that France is one of the least racist countries in the world are the product of men incapable of straight thinking.

In order to show us that racism does not reflect an economic situation, M. Mannoni reminds us that "in South Africa the white labourers are quite as racialist as the

2. My italics—F.F.

employers and managers and very often a good deal more so."[3]

I hope I may be forgiven for asking that those who take it on themselves to describe colonialism remember one thing: that it is utopian to try to ascertain in what ways one kind of inhuman behavior differs from another kind of inhuman behavior. I have no desire to add to the problems of the world, but I should simply like to ask M. Mannoni whether he does not think that for a Jew the differences between the anti-Semitism of Maurras and that of Goebbels are imperceptible.

After a presentation of *The Respectful Prostitute* in North Africa, a general remarked to Sartre: "It would be a good thing if your play could be put on in black Africa. It shows how much happier the black man is on French soil than his fellow Negroes are in America."

I sincerely believe that a subjective experience can be understood by others; and it would give me no pleasure to announce that the black problem is my problem and mine alone and that it is up to me to study it. But it does seem to me that M. Mannoni has not tried to feel himself into the despair of the man of color confronting the white man. In this work I have made it a point to convey the misery of the black man. Physically and affectively. I have not wished to be objective. Besides, that would be dishonest: It is not possible for me to be objective.

Is there in truth any difference between one racism and another? Do not all of them show the same collapse, the same bankruptcy of man?

M. Mannoni believes that the contempt of the poor whites of South Africa for the Negro has nothing to do with economic factors. Aside from the fact that this atti-

3. Mannoni, *op. cit.*, p. 24.

tude can be understood through the analogy of the anti-Semitic mentality—"Thus I would call anti-Semitism a poor man's snobbery. And in fact it would appear that the rich for the most part *exploit*[4] this passion for their own uses rather than abandon themselves to it—they have better things to do. It is propagated mainly among middle classes, because they possess neither land nor house nor castle. . . . By treating the Jew as an inferior and pernicious being, I affirm at the same time that I belong to the elite."[5]—we could point out to M. Mannoni that the displacement of the white proletariat's aggression on to the black proletariat is fundamentally a result of the economic structure of South Africa.

What is South Africa? A boiler into which thirteen million blacks are clubbed and penned in by two and a half million whites. If the poor whites hate the Negroes, it is not, as M. Mannoni would have us believe, because "racialism is the work of petty officials, small traders, and colonials who have toiled much without great success."[6] No; it is because the structure of South Africa is a racist structure:

> *Negrophilism* and *philanthropy* are pejoratives in South Africa . . . what is proposed is the separation of the natives from the Europeans, territorially, economically, and on the political level, allowing the blacks to build their own civilization under the guidance and the authority of the whites, but with a minimum of contact between the races. It is understood that territorial reservations would be set up for the blacks and that most of them would have to live there.

---

4. My italics—F.F.
5. Jean-Paul Sartre, *Anti-Semite and Jew* (New York, Grove Press, 1960), pp. 26-27. Originally, *Réflexions sur la question juive* (Paris, Morihien, 1946).
6. Mannoni, *op. cit.*, p. 24.

> . . . Economic competition would be eliminated and the groundwork would be laid *for the rehabilitation of the "poor whites" who constitute 50 per cent of the European population. . . .*
>
> It is no exaggeration to say that the majority of South Africans feel an almost physical revulsion against anything that puts a native or a person of color on their level.[7]

To conclude our consideration of M. Mannoni's thesis, let us remember that "economic exclusion results from, among other things, the fear of competition and the desire both to protect the poor-white class that forms half the European population and to prevent it from sinking any lower."

M. Mannoni adds: "Colonial exploitation is not the same as other forms of exploitation, and colonial racialism is different from other kinds of racialism. . . ."[8] He speaks of phenomenology, of psychoanalysis, of human brotherhood, but we should be happier if these terms had taken on a more concrete quality for him. All forms of exploitation resemble one another. They all seek the source of their necessity in some edict of a Biblical nature. All forms of exploitation are identical because all of them are applied against the same "object": man. When one tries to examine the structure of this or that form of exploitation from an abstract point of view, one simply turns one's back on the major, basic problem, which is that of restoring man to his proper place.

Colonial racism is no different from any other racism.

Anti-Semitism hits me head-on: I am enraged, I am bled white by an appalling battle, I am deprived of the

---

7. R. P. Oswin, Magrath of the Dominican Monastery of St. Nicholas, Stallenbosch, Republic of South Africa, *L'homme de* [illegible] My italics—F.F.

[illegible] *op. cit.*, p. 27.

possibility of being a man. I cannot disassociate myself from the future that is proposed for my brother. Every one of my acts commits me as a man. Every one of my silences, every one of my cowardices reveals me as a man.[9]

---

9. When I wrote this I had in mind Jaspers' concept of metaphysical guilt:

> There exists among men, because they are men, a solidarity through which each shares responsibility for every injustice and every wrong committed in the world, and especially for crimes that are committed in his presence or of which he cannot be ignorant. If I do not do whatever I can to prevent them, I am an accomplice in them. If I have not risked my life in order to prevent the murder of other men, if I have stood silent, I feel guilty in a sense that cannot in any adequate fashion be understood juridically, or politically, or morally. . . . That I am still alive after such things have been done weighs on me as a guilt that cannot be expiated.
>
> Somewhere in the heart of human relations an absolute command imposes itself: In case of criminal attack or of living conditions that threaten physical being, accept life only for all together, otherwise not at all. (Karl Jaspers, *La culpabilité allemande,* Jeanne Hersch's French translation, pp. 60-61.)

Jaspers declares that this obligation stems from God. It is easy to see that God has no business here. Unless one chooses not to state the obligation as the explicit human reality of feeling oneself responsible for one's fellow man. Responsible in the sense that the least of my actions involves all mankind. Every action is an answer or a question. Perhaps both. When I express a specific manner in which my being can rise above itself, I am affirming the worth of my action for others. Conversely, the passivity that is to be seen in troubled periods of history is to be interpreted as a default on that obligation. Jung, in *Aspects du drame contemporain,* says that, confronted by an Asiatic or a Hindu, every European has equally to answer for the crimes perpetrated by Nazi savagery. Another writer, Mme. Maryse Choisy, in *L'Anneau de Polycrate,* was able to describe the guilt of those who remained "neutral" during the occupation of France. In a confused way they felt that they were responsible for all the deaths and all the Buchenwalds.

I feel that I can still hear Césaire:

> When I turn on my radio, when I hear that Negroes have been lynched in America, I say that we have been lied to: Hitler is not dead; when I turn on my radio, when I learn that Jews have been insulted, mistreated, persecuted, I say that we have been lied to: Hitler is not dead; when, finally, I turn on my radio and hear that in Africa forced labor has been inaugurated and legalized, I say that we have certainly been lied to: Hitler is not dead.[10]

Yes, European civilization and its best representatives are responsible for colonial racism[11]; and I come back once more to Césaire:

> And then, one lovely day, the middle class is brought up short by a staggering blow: The Gestapos are busy again, the prisons are filling up, the torturers are once more inventing, perfecting, consulting over their workbenches.
>
> People are astounded, they are angry. They say: "How strange that is. But then it is only Nazism, it won't last." And they wait, and they hope; and they hide the truth from themselves: It is savagery, the supreme savagery, it crowns, it epitomizes the day-to-day savageries; yes, it is Nazism, but before they became its victims, they were its accomplices; that Nazism they tolerated before they succumbed to it, they exonerated it, they closed their eyes to it, they legitimated it because until then it had been employed only against non-European peoples; that Nazism they encouraged, they were responsible for it, and it drips, it seeps, it

---

10. Quoted from memory—*Discours politiques* of the election campaign of 1945, Fort-de-France.

11. "European civilization and its best representatives are not, for instance, responsible for colonial racialism; that is the work of petty officials, small traders, and colonials who have toiled much without great success" (Mannoni, p. 24).

> wells from every crack in western Christian civilization until it engulfs that civilization in a bloody sea.[12]

Whenever I see an Arab with his hunted look, suspicious, on the run, wrapped in those long ragged robes that seem to have been created especially for him, I say to myself, "M. Mannoni was wrong." Many times I have been stopped in broad daylight by policemen who mistook me for an Arab; when they discovered my origins, they were obsequious in their apologies; "Of course we know that a Martinican is quite different from an Arab." I always protested violently, but I was always told, "You don't know them." Indeed, M. Mannoni, you are wrong. For what is the meaning of this sentence: "European civilization and its best representatives are not responsible for colonial racialism"? What does it mean except that colonialism is the business of adventurers and politicians, the "best representatives" remaining well above the battle? But, Francis Jeanson says, every citizen of a nation is responsible for the actions committed in the name of that nation:

> Day after day, that system elaborates its evil projects in your presence, day after day its leaders betray you, pursuing, in the name of France, a policy as foreign as possible not only to your real interests but also to your deepest needs. . . . You pride yourselves on keeping your distance from realities of a certain kind: so you allow a free hand to those who are immune to the most unhealthy climates because they create these climates themselves through their own conduct. And if, apparently, you succeed in keeping yourselves unsullied, it is because others dirty themselves in your place. *You hire thugs,* and, balancing the accounts, it is you who are the real criminals: for without you, with-

12. Aimé Césaire, *Discours sur le colonialisme* (Paris, Présence Africaine, 1956), pp. 14-15.

out your blind indifference, such men could never carry out deeds that damn you as much as they shame those men.[13]

I said just above that South Africa has a racist structure. Now I shall go farther and say that Europe has a racist structure. It is plain to see that M. Mannoni has no interest in this problem, for he says, "France is unquestionably one of the least racialist-minded countries in the world."[14] Be glad that you are French, my fine Negro friends, even if it is a little hard, for your counterparts in America are much worse off than you. . . . France is a racist country, for the myth of the bad nigger is part of the collective unconscious. We shall demonstrate this presently (Chapter Six).

But let us proceed with M. Mannoni: "In practice, therefore, an inferiority complex connected with the colour of the skin is found only among those who form a minority within a group of another colour. In a fairly homogeneous community like that of the Malagasies, where the social framework is still fairly strong, an inferiority complex occurs only in very exceptional cases." [15]

Once again one asks the author to be somewhat more careful. A white man in a colony has never felt inferior in any respect; as M. Mannoni expresses it so well, "He will be deified or devoured." The colonial, even though he is "in the minority," does not feel that this makes him inferior. In Martinique there are two hundred whites who consider themselves superior to 300,000 people of color. In South Africa there are two million whites against almost thirteen million native people, and it has never

13. Francis Jeanson, "Cette Algérie conquise et pacifiée . . . ," in *Esprit,* April, 1950, p. 624.

14. Mannoni, *op. cit.*, p. 110.

15. *Ibid.*, p. 39.

occurred to a single black to consider himself superior to a member of the white minority.

While the discoveries of Adler and the no less interesting findings of Kuenkel explain certain kinds of neurotic behavior, one cannot infer from them laws that would apply to immeasurably complex problems. The feeling of inferiority of the colonized is the correlative to the European's feeling of superiority. Let us have the courage to say it outright: *It is the racist who creates his inferior.*

This conclusion brings us back to Sartre: "The Jew is one whom other men consider a Jew: that is the simple truth from which we must start. . . . It is the anti-Semite who *makes* the Jew."[16]

What becomes of the exceptional cases of which M. Mannoni tells us? Quite simply, they are the instances in which the educated Negro suddenly discovers that he is rejected by a civilization which he has none the less assimilated. So that the conclusion would come to this: To the extent to which M. Mannoni's real typical Malagasy takes on "dependent behavior," all is for the best; if, however, he forgets his place, if he takes it into his head to be the equal of the European, then the said European is indignant and casts out the upstart—who, in such circumstance, in this "exceptional case," pays for his own rejection of dependence with an inferiority complex.

Earlier, we uncovered in certain of M. Mannoni's statements a mistake that is at the very least dangerous. In effect, he leaves the Malagasy no choice save between inferiority and dependence. These two solutions excepted, there is no salvation. "When he [the Malagasy] has succeeded in forming such relations [of dependence] with

---

16. Sartre, *Anti-Semite*, p. 69.

his superiors, his inferiority no longer troubles him: everything is all right. When he fails to establish them, when his feeling of insecurity is not assuaged in this way, he suffers a crisis."[17]

The primary concern of M. Mannoni was to criticize the methods hitherto employed by the various ethnographers who had turned their attention to primitive peoples. But we see the criticism that must be made of his own work.

After having sealed the Malagasy into his own customs, after having evolved a unilateral analysis of his view of the world, after having described the Malagasy within a closed circle, after having noted that the Malagasy has a dependency relation toward his ancestors—a strong tribal characteristic—M. Mannoni, in defiance of all objectivity, applies his conclusions to a bilateral totality—deliberately ignoring the fact that, since Galliéni,[18] *the Malagasy has ceased to exist.*

What we wanted from M. Mannoni was an explanation of the colonial situation. He notably overlooked providing it. Nothing has been lost, nothing has been gained, we agree. Parodying Hegel, Georges Balandier said of the

---

17. Mannoni, *op. cit.*, pp. 61-62.

18. General Joseph-Simon Galliéni, "the hero of the Marne," played a major part in French colonial expansion. After his conquests in Africa and his service on Martinique, he was appointed resident-general of Madagascar in 1896, when it was made a French colony, and he later became governor-general. According to the Encyclopaedia Britannica (fourteenth edition), "He completed the subjugation of the island, which was in revolt against the French. . . . His policy was directed to the development of the economic resources of the island and was conciliatory toward the non-French *European* population." (Translator's note.)

dynamics of the personality, in an essay[19] devoted to Kardiner and Linton: "The last of its stages is the result of all its preceding stages and should contain all their elements." It is whimsical, but it is the principle that guides many scholars. The reactions and the behavior patterns to which the arrival of the European in Madagascar gave rise were not tacked on to a pre-existing set. There was no addition to the earlier psychic whole. If, for instance, Martians undertook to colonize the earth men—not to initiate them into Martian culture but to *colonize* them—we should be doubtful of the persistence of any earth personality. Kardiner changed many opinions when he wrote: "To teach Christianity to the people of Alor would be a quixotic undertaking. . . . [It] would make no sense inasmuch as one would be dealing with personalities built out of elements that are in complete disaccord with Christian doctrine: It would certainly be starting out at the wrong end."[20] And if Negroes are impervious to the teachings of Christ, this is not at all because they are incapable of assimilating them. To understand something new requires that we make ourselves ready for it, that we prepare ourselves for it; it entails the shaping of a new form. It is utopian to expect the Negro or the Arab to exert the effort of embedding abstract values into his outlook on the world when he has barely enough food to keep alive. To ask a Negro of the Upper Niger to wear shoes, to say of him that he will never be a Schubert, is no less ridiculous than to be surprised that a worker in the Berliet truck factory does not spend his evenings studying lyricism in Hindu literature

19. "Où l'ethnologie retrouve l'unité de l'homme," in *Esprit*, April, 1950.

20. Quoted by Georges Balandier, *ibid.*, p. 610.

or to say that he will never be an Einstein.

Actually, in the absolute sense, nothing stands in the way of such things. Nothing—except that the people in question lack the opportunities.

But they do not complain! Here is the proof:

> At the hour before dawn, on the far side of my father and my mother, the whole hut cracking and blistered, like a sinner punished with boils, and the weather-worn roof patched here and there with pieces of gasoline tins, and this leaves bogs of rust in the dirty gray stinking mud that holds the straw together, and, when the wind blows, all this patchwork makes strange sounds, first like something sizzling in a frying pan and then like a flaming board hurled into water in a shower of flying sparks. And the bed of planks from which my race has risen, all my race from this bed of planks on its feet of kerosene cases, as if the old bed had elephantiasis, covered with a goat skin, and its dried banana leaves and its rags, the ghost of a mattress that is my grandmother's bed (above the bed in a pot full of oil a candle-end whose flame looks like a fat turnip, and on the side of the pot, in letters of gold: MERCI).[21]

Wretchedly,

> this attitude, this behavior, this shackled life caught in the noose of shame and disaster rebels, hates itself, struggles, howls, and, my God, others ask: "What can you do about it?"
>
> "Start something!"
>
> "Start what?"
>
> "The only thing in the world that's worth the effort of starting: The end of the world, by God!"[22]

What M. Mannoni has forgotten is that the Malagasy

21. Aimé Césaire, *Cahier d'un retour au pays natal* (Paris, Présence Africaine, 1956), p. 56.

22. *Ibid.*

alone no longer exists; he has forgotten that the Malagasy exists *with the European*. The arrival of the white man in Madagascar shattered not only its horizons but its psychological mechanisms. As everyone has pointed out, alterity for the black man is not the black but the white man. An island like Madagascar, invaded overnight by "pioneers of civilization," even if those pioneers conducted themselves as well as they knew how, suffered the loss of its basic structure. M. Mannoni himself, furthermore, says as much: "The petty kings were all very anxious to get possession of a white man."[23] Explain that as one may in terms of magical-totemic patterns, of a need for contact with an awesome God, of its proof of a system of dependency, the fact still remains that something new had come into being on that island and that it had to be reckoned with—otherwise the analysis is condemned to falsehood, to absurdity, to nullity. A new element having been introduced, it became mandatory to seek to understand the new relationships.

The landing of the white man on Madagascar inflicted injury without measure. The consequences of that irruption of Europeans onto Madagascar were not psychological alone, since, as every authority has observed, there are inner relationships between consciousness and the social context.

And the economic consequences? Why, colonization itself must be brought to trial!

Let us go on with our study.

> In other words, the Malagasy can bear not being a white man; what hurts him cruelly is to have discovered first (by identification) that he is a man and *later* that men are divided into whites and blacks. If the "abandoned" or "be-

23. Mannoni, *op. cit.*, p. 80.

trayed" Malagasy continues his identification, he becomes clamorous; he begins to demand *equality* in a way he had never before found necessary. The equality he seeks would have been beneficial before he started asking for it, but afterwards it proves inadequate to remedy his ills—for every increase in equality makes the remaining differences seem the more intolerable, for they suddenly appear agonizingly irremovable. This is the road along which [the Malagasy] passes from psychological dependence to psychological inferiority.[24]

Here again we encounter the same misapprehension. It is of course obvious that the Malagasy can perfectly well tolerate the fact of not being a white man. A Malagasy is a Malagasy; or, rather, no, not he *is* a Malagasy but, rather, in an absolute sense he "lives" his Malagasyhood. If he is a Malagasy, it is because the white man has come, and if at a certain stage he has been led to ask himself whether he is indeed a man, it is because his reality as a man has been challenged. In other words, I begin to suffer from not being a white man to the degree that the white man imposes discrimination on me, makes me a colonized native, robs me of all worth, all individuality, tells me that I am a parasite on the world, that I must bring myself as quickly as possible into step with the white world, "that I am a brute beast, that my people and I are like a walking dung-heap that disgustingly fertilizes sweet sugar cane and silky cotton, that I have no use in the world."[25] Then I will quite simply try to make myself white: that is, I will compel the white man to acknowledge that I am human. But, M. Mannoni will counter, you cannot do it, because in your depths there is a dependency complex.

"Not all peoples can be colonized; only those who expe-

24. *Ibid.*, p. 84.
25. Césaire, *Cahier d'un retour.*

rience this need [for dependency]." And, a little later: "Wherever Europeans have founded colonies of the type we are considering, it can safely be said that their coming was unconsciously expected—even desired—by the future subject peoples. Everywhere there existed legends foretelling the arrival of strangers from the sea, bearing wondrous gifts with them."[26] It becomes obvious that the white man acts in obedience to an authority complex, a leadership complex, while the Malagasy obeys a dependency complex. Everyone is satisfied.

When the question arises of understanding why the European, the foreigner, was called *vazaha,* which means *honorable stranger;* when it is a matter of understanding why shipwrecked Europeans were welcomed with open arms; why the European, the foreigner, was never thought of as an enemy, instead of explaining these things in terms of humanity, of good will, of courtesy, basic characteristics of what Césaire calls "the old courtly civilizations," scholars tell us that it happened quite simply because, inscribed in "fateful hieroglyphics"—specifically, the unconscious—there exists something that makes the white man the awaited master. Yes, the unconscious—we have got to that. But one must not extrapolate. A Negro tells me his dream: "I had been walking for a long time, I was extremely exhausted, I had the impression that something was waiting for me, I climbed barricades and walls, I came into an empty hall, and from behind a door I heard noise. I hesitated before I went in, but finally I made up my mind and opened the door. In this second room there were white men, and I found that I too was white." When I try to understand this dream, to analyze it, knowing that my friend has had problems in his career, I conclude that

---

26. Mannoni, *op. cit.*, pp. 85-86.

this dream fulfills an unconscious wish. But when, outside my psychoanalytic office, I have to incorporate my conclusions into the context of the world, I will assert:

1. My patient is suffering from an inferiority complex. His psychic structure is in danger of disintegration. What has to be done is to save him from this and, little by little, to rid him of this unconscious desire.

2. If he is overwhelmed to such a degree by the wish to be white, it is because he lives in a society that makes his inferiority complex possible, in a society that derives its stability from the perpetuation of this complex, in a society that proclaims the superiority of one race; to the identical degree to which that society creates difficulties for him, he will find himself thrust into a neurotic situation.

What emerges then is the need for combined action on the individual and on the group. As a psychoanalyst, I should help my patient to become *conscious* of his unconscious and abandon his attempts at a hallucinatory whitening, but also to act in the direction of a change in the social structure.

In other words, the black man should no longer be confronted by the dilemma, *turn white or disappear;* but he should be able to take cognizance of a possibility of existence. In still other words, if society makes difficulties for him because of his color, if in his dreams I establish the expression of an unconscious desire to change color, my objective will not be that of dissuading him from it by advising him to "keep his place"; on the contrary, my objective, once his motivations have been brought into consciousness, will be to put him in a position to *choose* action (or passivity) with respect to the real source of the conflict—that is, toward the social structures.

Conscientious in his desire to examine the problem from every angle, M. Mannoni has not overlooked the investigation of the unconscious of the Malagasy. To this end he analyzes seven dreams: seven narratives that open the unconscious to us, and in six of them we find a dominant theme of terror. Six children and an adult tell us their dreams, and we see them trembling, seeking flight, unhappy.

The cook's dream. "I was being chased by an angry *black*[27] bull. Terrified, I climbed up into a tree and stayed there till the danger was past. I came down again, trembling all over." . . .

Dream of a thirteen-year-old boy, Rahevi. "While going for a walk in the woods, I met two *black*[28] men. 'Oh,' I though, 'I am done for!' I tried to run away but couldn't. They barred my way and began jabbering in a strange tongue. I thought they were saying, 'We'll show you what death is.' I shivered with fright and begged, 'Please, Sirs, let me go, I'm so frightened.' One of them understood French but in spite of that they said, 'We are going to take you to our chief.' As we set off they made me go in front and they showed me their rifles. I was more frightened than ever, but before reaching their camp we had to cross a river. I dived deep into the water and thanks to my presence of mind found a rocky cave where I hid. When the two men had gone I ran back to my parents' house." . . .

Josette's dream. The dreamer, a young girl, got lost and sat down on a fallen tree-trunk. A woman in a white dress told her that she was in the midst of a band of robbers. The account goes on: " 'I am a schoolgirl,' I said, trembling, 'and I lost my way here when I was going home from school,' and she replied: 'Follow this path, child, and you will find your way home.' " . . .

Dream of a fourteen-year-old boy, Razafi. He is being chased by (Senegalese) soldiers who "make a noise like

27. My italics—F.F.
28. My italics—F.F.

galloping horses as they run," and "show their rifles in front of them." The dreamer escapes by becoming invisible; he climbs a stairway and finds the door of his home. . . .

Dream of Elphine, a girl of thirteen or fourteen. "I dreamed that a fierce *black*[29] ox was chasing me. He was big and strong. On his head, which was almost mottled (*sic*) with white he had two long horns with sharp points. 'Oh how dreadful,' I thought. The path was getting narrower. What should I do? I perched myself in a mango tree, but the ox rent its trunk. Alas, I fell among the bushes. Then he pressed his horns into me; my stomach fell out and he devoured it." . . .

Raza's dream. In his dream the boy heard someone say at school that the Senegalese were coming. "I went out of the school yard to see." The Senegalese were indeed coming. He ran home. "But our house had been dispersed by them too." . . .

Dream of a fourteen-year-old boy, Si. "I was walking in the garden and felt something like a shadow behind me. All around me the leaves were rustling and falling off, as if a robber was in hiding among them, waiting to catch me. Wherever I walked, up and down the alleys, the shadow still followed me. Suddenly I got frightened and started running, but the shadow took great strides and stretched out his huge hand to take hold of my clothes. I felt my shirt tearing, and screamed. My father jumped out of bed when he heard me scream and came over to look at me, but the big *shadow*[30] had disappeared and I was no longer afraid."[31]

Some ten years ago I was astonished to learn that the North Africans despised men of color. It was absolutely impossible for me to make any contact with the local population. I left Africa and went back to France without

---

29. My italics—F.F.
30. My italics—F.F.
31. Mannoni, *op. cit.*, pp. 89-92.

having fathomed the reason for this hostility. Meanwhile, certain facts had made me think. The Frenchman does not like the Jew, who does not like the Arab, who does not like the Negro. . . . The Arab is told: "If you are poor, it is because the Jew has bled you and taken everything from you." The Jew is told: "You are not of the same class as the Arab because you are really white and because you have Einstein and Bergson." The Negro is told: "You are the best soldiers in the French Empire; the Arabs think they are better than you, but they are wrong." But that is not true; the Negro is told nothing because no one has anything to tell him, the Senegalese trooper is a trooper, the-good-soldier-under-command, the brave fellow-who-only-knows-how-to-obey.

"You no come in."

"Why not?"

"Me not know. You no come in."

Unable to stand up to all the demands, the white man sloughs off his responsibilities. I have a name for this procedure: the racial distribution of guilt.

I have remarked that certain things surprised me. Whenever there has been any attempt at insurrection, the military authorities have ordered only colored soldiers into action. They were "men of color" who nullified the liberation efforts of other "men of color," proof that there was no reason to universalize the procedure: If those good-for-nothings, the Arabs, took it into their heads to revolt, it was not in the name of any acceptable principle but purely and simply in order to get rid of their *"bicot"* unconscious.

From the African point of view, a colored student said at the 25th Congress of Catholic Students during its discussion of Madagascar, "I wish to protest against the dispatch of Senegalese troops there and the misuse that is being made of them." We know from other sources that one of the torturers in the Tananarive police headquarters was a Senegalese. Therefore, since we know all this, since we know what the archetype of the Senegalese can represent for the Malagasy, the discoveries of Freud are of no use to us here. What must be done is to restore this dream *to its proper time,* and this time is the period during which eighty thousand natives were killed—that is to say, one of every fifty persons in the population; and *to its proper place,* and this place is an island of four million people, at the center of which no real relationship can be established, where dissension breaks out in every direction, where the only masters are lies and demagogy.[32] One

---

32. We bring up in this connection the following testimony given at a trial in Tananarive.

(Session of August 9. Rakotovao states:)

M. Baron said to me, "Since you refuse to accept what I just told you, I'm sending you to the 'thinking room.' . . ." I was led into the adjoining chamber. The floor of the room in question was already covered with water. There was a pail full of dirty water, not to mention other things. M. Baron said to me, "Now you'll learn to agree to what I said you should declare." He gave an order to a Senegalese to "do the same to me as to the others." The Senegalese made me kneel with my wrists facing outward; then he took wooden tongs and squeezed my hands together; then, with me kneeling and my two hands pressed together, he put his foot on the back of my neck and forced my head down into the bucket. Seeing that I was on the point of fainting, he removed his foot so that I could get some air. And this was repeated again and again until I was completely exhausted. Then M. Baron said, "Take him away and beat him." The Senegalese thereupon used a bull-whip, but M. Baron came into the torture chamber and personally took part in the whipping. This went on for about fifteen minutes, I think, after which I said that I couldn't endure any more, because in spite of my youth it was unbearable. Then he said, "In that case you must agree to what I told you before!"

must concede that in some circumstances the *socius* is more important than the individual. I recall what Pierre Naville wrote:

"No, *Monsieur le directeur,* it is not true."

Thereupon he sent me back into the first torture chamber and called in another Senegalese, since one was not enough, and he ordered them to hold me up by the feet and lower me into the bucket as far as my chest. This they did several times. Finally I told them, "It's too much! Let me talk to M. Baron," and to him I said, "I request at least that I be treated in a manner befitting France, *Monsieur le directeur,*" to which he replied, "You're getting French treatment!"

Since I could stand no more, I said to him, "All right, I'll accept the first part of your statement." M. Baron replied, "No, I don't want the first part, I want it all." "Am I supposed to lie, then?" "Lie or no lie, you must agree to what I tell you. . . ."

(The testimony went on:)

Immediately M. Baron said, "Try some other method on him." I was then taken back into the adjoining room, where there was a small stone stairway. My arms were tied behind me. The two Senegalese again held me with my feet in the air and made me go up and down the stairs in this way. This was beginning to be unendurable, and, even if I had had any moral strength left, it was physically too much. I said to the Senegalese, "Tell your boss I'll agree to what he wants me to say."

(In the session of August 11, Robert, a defendant, testified:)

The policeman took me by my shirt collar and kicked me in the behind and punched me in the face. Then he forced me to kneel, and M. Baron began hitting me again.

Without my knowing how he managed it, he got behind me and I felt hot irons against the back of my neck. I tried to protect myself with my hands and they were burned too. . . .

The third time I was knocked down I lost consciousness and I don't know any more what happened. M. Baron told me to sign a paper that was all ready; I shook my head *no;* then the director called the Senegalese in again and he half-carried me into another torture chamber. "You better give in or you'll be dead," the Senegalese said. The director said, "That's his lookout, you have to get started, Jean." My arms were tied behind my

To speak of society's dreams as one speaks of the dreams of the individual, to discuss collective will to power as one discusses individual sexual drive, is to reverse the natural order of things once more, because, on the contrary, it is the economic and social conditions of class conflicts that explain and determine the real conditions in which individual sexuality expresses itself, and because the content of a human being's dreams depends also, in the last analysis, on the general conditions of the culture in which he lives."[33]

The enraged black bull is not the phallus. The two black men are not the two father figures—the one standing for the real father, the other for the primal ancestor. Here is what a thorough analysis could have found, on the same basis of M. Mannoni's conclusions in his section, "The Cult of the Dead and the Family."

The rifle of the Senegalese soldier is not a penis but a genuine rifle, model Lebel 1916. The black bull and the robber are not *lolos*—"reincarnated souls"—but actually the irruption of real fantasies into sleep. What does this stereotype, this central theme of the dreams, represent if not a return to the right road? Sometimes we have *black* soldiers, sometimes *black* bulls speckled with white at the head, sometimes, outright, a white woman who is

---

back, I was forced down on my knees, and my head was pushed into a bucket full of water. Just as I was about to suffocate I was pulled out. Then they did the same thing over and over again until I passed out completely. . . .

Let us recall, so that no one may plead ignorance of the fact, that the witness Rakotovao was sentenced to death.

So, when one reads such things, it certainly seems that M. Mannoni allowed one aspect of the phenomena that he analyzes to escape him: The black bull and the black men are neither more nor less than the Senegalese police torturers.

33. *Psychologie, Marxisme, Matérialisme*, 2nd ed. (Paris, Marcel Rivière, 1948), p. 151.

quite kind. What do we find in all these dreams if not this central idea: "To depart from routine is to wander in pathless woods; there you will meet the bull who will send you running helter-skelter home again."[34]

Settle down, Malagasies, and stay where you belong.

After having described the Malagasy psychology, M. Mannoni takes it upon himself to explain colonialism's reason for existence. In the process he adds a new complex to the standing catalogue: the "Prospero complex." It is defined as the sum of those unconscious neurotic tendencies that delineate at the same time the "picture" of the paternalist colonial and the portrait of "the racialist whose daughter has suffered an [imaginary] attempted rape at the hands of an inferior being."[35]

Prospero, as we know, is the main character of Shakespeare's comedy, *The Tempest.* Opposite him we have his daughter, Miranda, and Caliban. Toward Caliban, Prospero assumes an attitude that is well known to Americans in the southern United States. Are they not forever saying that the niggers are just waiting for the chance to jump on white women? In any case, what is interesting in this part of his book is the intensity with which M. Mannoni makes us feel the ill-resolved conflicts that seem to be at the root of the colonial vocation. In effect, he tells us:

> What the colonial in common with Prospero lacks, is awareness of the world of Others, a world in which Others have to be respected. This is the world from which the colonial has fled because he cannot accept men as they are. Rejection

34. Mannoni, *op. cit.*, p. 70.
35. *Ibid.*, p. 110.

> of that world is combined with an urge to dominate, an urge which is infantile in origin and which social adaptation has failed to discipline. The reason the colonial himself gives for his flight—whether he says it was the desire to travel, or the desire to escape from the cradle or from the "ancient parapets," or whether he says that he simply wanted a freer life—is of no consequence. . . . It is always a question of compromising with the desire for a world without men.[36]

If one adds that many Europeans go to the colonies because it is possible for them to grow rich quickly there, that with rare exceptions the colonial is a merchant, or rather a trafficker, one will have grasped the psychology of the man who arouses in the autochthonous population "the feeling of inferiority." As for the Malagasy "dependency complex," at least in the only form in which we can reach it and analyze it, it too proceeds from the arrival of white colonizers on the island. From its other form, from this original complex in its pure state that supposedly characterized the Malagasy mentality throughout the whole precolonial period, it appears to me that M. Mannoni lacks the slightest basis on which to ground any conclusion applicable to the situation, the problems, or the potentialities of the Malagasy in the present time.

36. *Ibid.*, p. 108.

Chapter Five

THE FACT OF BLACKNESS

"Dirty nigger!" Or simply, "Look, a Negro!"

I came into the world imbued with the will to find a meaning in things, my spirit filled with the desire to attain to the source of the world, and then I found that I was an object in the midst of other objects.

Sealed into that crushing objecthood, I turned beseechingly to others. Their attention was a liberation, running over my body suddenly abraded into nonbeing, endowing me once more with an agility that I had thought lost, and by taking me out of the world, restoring me to it. But just as I reached the other side, I stumbled, and the movements, the attitudes, the glances of the other fixed me there, in the sense in which a chemical solution is fixed by a dye. I was indignant; I demanded an explanation. Nothing happened. I burst apart. Now the fragments have been put together again by another self.

As long as the black man is among his own, he will have no occasion, except in minor internal conflicts, to experience his being through others. There is of course the moment of "being for others," of which Hegel speaks, but every ontology is made unattainable in a colonized and civilized society. It would seem that this fact has not been given sufficient attention by those who have discussed the question. In the *Weltanschauung* of a colonized people there is an impurity, a flaw that outlaws any ontological explanation. Someone may object that this is the case with every individual, but such an objection merely conceals a basic problem. Ontology—once it is finally admitted as leaving existence by the wayside—does not permit us to understand the being of the black man. For not only must the black man be black; he must be black in relation to the white man. Some critics will take it on themselves to remind us that this proposition has a converse. I say that this is false. The black man has no ontological resistance in the eyes of the white man. Overnight the Negro has been given two frames of reference within which he has had to place himself. His metaphysics, or, less pretentiously, his customs and the sources on which they were based, were wiped out because they were in conflict with a civilization that he did not know and that imposed itself on him.

The black man among his own in the twentieth century does not know at what moment his inferiority comes into being through the other. Of course I have talked about the black problem with friends, or, more rarely, with American Negroes. Together we protested, we asserted the equality of all men in the world. In the Antilles there was also that little gulf that exists among the almost-white, the mulatto, and the nigger. But I was satisfied with an intellectual understanding of these differences. It was not really dramatic. And then. . . .

And then the occasion arose when I had to meet the white man's eyes. An unfamiliar weight burdened me. The real world challenged my claims. In the white world the man of color encounters difficulties in the development of his bodily schema. Consciousness of the body is solely a negating activity. It is a third-person consciousness. The body is surrounded by an atmosphere of certain uncertainty. I know that if I want to smoke, I shall have to reach out my right arm and take the pack of cigarettes lying at the other end of the table. The matches, however, are in the drawer on the left, and I shall have to lean back slightly. And all these movements are made not out of habit but out of implicit knowledge. A slow composition of my *self* as a body in the middle of a spatial and temporal world—such seems to be the schema. It does not impose itself on me; it is, rather, a definitive structuring of the self and of the world—definitive because it creates a real dialectic between my body and the world.

For several years certain laboratories have been trying to produce a serum for "denegrification"; with all the earnestness in the world, laboratories have sterilized their test tubes, checked their scales, and embarked on researches that might make it possible for the miserable Negro to whiten himself and thus to throw off the burden of that corporeal malediction. Below the corporeal schema I had sketched a historico-racial schema. The elements that I used had been provided for me not by "residual sensations and perceptions primarily of a tactile, vestibular, kinesthetic, and visual character,"[1] but by the other, the white man, who had woven me out of a thousand details, anecdotes, stories. I thought that what I had in hand was to construct a physiological self, to balance space, to localize sensations, and here I was called on for more.

"Look, a Negro!" It was an external stimulus that flicked over me as I passed by. I made a tight smile.

"Look, a Negro!" It was true. It amused me.

---

1. Jean Lhermitte, *L'Image de notre corps* (Paris, Nouvelle Revue critique, 1939), p. 17.

"Look, a Negro!" The circle was drawing a bit tighter. I made no secret of my amusement.

"Mama, see the Negro! I'm frightened!" Frightened! Frightened! Now they were beginning to be afraid of me. I made up my mind to laugh myself to tears, but laughter had become impossible.

I could no longer laugh, because I already knew that there were legends, stories, history, and above all *historicity,* which I had learned about from Jaspers. Then, assailed at various points, the corporeal schema crumbled, its place taken by a racial epidermal schema. In the train it was no longer a question of being aware of my body in the third person but in a triple person. In the train I was given not one but two, three places. I had already stopped being amused. It was not that I was finding febrile coordinates in the world. I existed triply: I occupied space. I moved toward the other . . . and the evanescent other, hostile but not opaque, transparent, not there, disappeared. Nausea. . . .

I was responsible at thc same time for my body, for my race, for my ancestors. I subjected myself to an objective examination, I discovered my blackness, my ethnic characteristics; and I was battered down by tom-toms, cannibalism, intellectual deficiency, fetichism, racial defects, slave-ships, and above all else, above all: "Sho' good eatin'."

On that day, completely dislocated, unable to be abroad with the other, the white man, who unmercifully imprisoned me, I took myself far off from my own presence, far indeed, and made myself an object. What else could it be for me but an amputation, an excision, a hemorrhage that spattered my whole body with black blood? But I did not want this revision, this thematization. All I wanted was to be a man among other men. I wanted to come lithe and young into a world that was ours and to help to build it together.

But I rejected all immunization of the emotions. I wanted to be a man, nothing but a man. Some identified me with ancestors of mine who had been enslaved or lynched: I decided to accept this. It was on the universal level of the intellect that I understood this inner kinship —I was the grandson of slaves in exactly the same way in which President Lebrun was the grandson of tax-paying, hard-working peasants. In the main, the panic soon vanished.

In America, Negroes are segregated. In South America, Negroes are whipped in the streets, and Negro strikers are cut down by machine-guns. In West Africa, the Negro is an animal. And there beside me, my neighbor in the university, who was born in Algeria, told me: "As long as the Arab is treated like a man, no solution is possible."

"Understand, my dear boy, color prejudice is something I find utterly foreign. . . . But of course, come in, sir, there is no color prejudice among us. . . . Quite, the Negro is a man like ourselves. . . . It is not because he is black that he is less intelligent than we are. . . . I had a Senegalese buddy in the army who was really clever. . . ."

Where am I to be classified? Or, if you prefer, tucked away?

"A Martinican, a native of 'our' old colonies."

Where shall I hide?

"Look at the nigger! . . . Mama, a Negro! . . . Hell, he's getting mad. . . . Take no notice, sir, he does not know that you are as civilized as we. . . ."

My body was given back to me sprawled out, distorted, recolored, clad in mourning in that white winter day. The Negro is an animal, the Negro is bad, the Negro is mean, the Negro is ugly; look, a nigger, it's cold, the nigger is shivering, the nigger is shivering because he is cold, the little boy is trembling because he is afraid of the nigger, the nigger is shivering with cold, that cold that goes through your bones, the handsome little boy is trembling because he thinks that the nigger is quivering with rage, the little white boy throws himself into his mother's arms: Mama, the nigger's going to eat me up.

All round me the white man, above the sky tears at its navel, the earth rasps under my feet, and there is a white song, a white song. All this whiteness that burns me. . . .

I sit down at the fire and I become aware of my uniform. I had not seen it. It is indeed ugly. I stop there, for who can tell me what beauty is?

Where shall I find shelter from now on? I felt an easily identifiable flood mounting out of the countless facets of my being. I was about to be angry. The fire was long since out, and once more the nigger was trembling.

"Look how handsome that Negro is! . . ."

"Kiss the handsome Negro's ass, madame!"

Shame flooded her face. At last I was set free from my rumination. At the same time I accomplished two things: I identified my enemies and I made a scene. A grand slam. Now one would be able to laugh.

The field of battle having been marked out, I entered the lists.

What? While I was forgetting, forgiving, and wanting only to love, my message was flung back in my face like a slap. The white world, the only honorable one, barred me from all participation. A man was expected to behave like a man. I was expected to behave like a black man—or at least like a nigger. I shouted a greeting to the world and the world slashed away my joy. I was told to stay within bounds, to go back where I belonged.

They would see, then! I had warned them, anyway. Slavery? It was no longer even mentioned, that unpleasant memory. My supposed inferiority? A hoax that it was better to laugh at. I forgot it all, but only on condition that the world not protect itself against me any longer. I had incisors to test. I was sure they were strong. And besides. . . .

What! When it was I who had every reason to hate, to despise, I was rejected? When I should have been begged, implored, I was denied the slightest recognition? I resolved, since it was impossible for me to get away from an *inborn complex*, to assert myself as a BLACK MAN. Since the other hesitated to recognize me, there remained only one solution: to make myself known.

In *Anti-Semite and Jew* (p. 95), Sartre says: "They [the Jews] have allowed themselves to be poisoned by the stereotype that others have of them, and they live in fear that their acts will correspond to this stereotype. . . . We may say that their conduct is perpetually overdetermined from the inside."

All the same, the Jew can be unknown in his Jewishness. He is not wholly what he is. One hopes, one waits. His actions, his behavior are the final determinant. He is a white man, and, apart from some rather debatable characteristics, he can sometimes go unnoticed. He belongs to the race of those who since the beginning of time have never known cannibalism. What an idea, to eat one's father! Simple enough, one has only not to be a nigger. Granted, the Jews are harassed—what am I thinking of? They are hunted down, exterminated, cremated. But these are little family quarrels. The Jew is disliked from the moment he is tracked down. But in my case everything takes on a *new* guise. I am given no chance. I am overdetermined from without. I am the slave not of the "idea" that others have of me but of my own appearance.

I move slowly in the world, accustomed now to seek no longer for upheaval. I progress by crawling. And already I am being dissected under white eyes, the only real eyes. I am *fixed*. Having adjusted their microtomes, they objectively cut away slices of my reality. I am laid bare. I feel, I see in those white faces that it is not a new man who has come in, but a new kind of man, a new genus. Why, it's a Negro!

I slip into corners, and my long antennae pick up the catch-phrases strewn over the surface of things—nigger underwear smells of nigger—nigger teeth are white—nigger feet are big—the nigger's barrel chest—I slip into corners, I remain silent, I strive for anonymity, for invisibility. Look, I will accept the lot, as long as no one notices me!

"Oh, I want you to meet my black friend. . . . Aimé Césaire, a black man and a university graduate. . . . Marian Anderson, the finest of Negro singers. . . . Dr. Cobb, who invented white blood, is a Negro. . . . Here, say hello to my friend from Martinique (be careful, he's extremely sensitive). . . ."

Shame. Shame and self-contempt. Nausea. When people like me, they tell me it is in spite of my color. When they dislike me, they point out that it is not because of my color. Either way, I am locked into the infernal circle.

I turn away from these inspectors of the Ark before the Flood and I attach myself to my brothers, Negroes like myself. To my horror, they too reject me. They are almost white. And besides they are about to marry white women. They will have children faintly tinged with brown. Who knows, perhaps little by little. . . .

I had been dreaming.

"I want you to understand, sir, I am one of the best friends the Negro has in Lyon."

The evidence was there, unalterable. My blackness was there, dark and unarguable. And it tormented me, pursued me, disturbed me, angered me.

Negroes are savages, brutes, illiterates. But in my own case I knew that these statements were false. There was a myth of the Negro that had to be destroyed at all costs. The time had long since passed when a Negro priest was an occasion for wonder. We had physicians, professors, statesmen. Yes, but something out of the ordinary still clung to such cases. "We have a Senegalese history teacher. He is quite bright. . . . Our doctor is colored. He is very gentle."

It was always the Negro teacher, the Negro doctor; brittle as I was becoming, I shivered at the slightest pretext. I knew, for instance, that if the physician made a mistake it would be the end of him and of all those who came after him. What could one expect, after all, from a Negro physician? As long as everything went well, he was praised to the skies, but look out, no nonsense, under any conditions! The black physician can never be sure how close he is to disgrace. I tell you, I was walled in: No exception was made for my refined manners, or my knowledge of literature, or my understanding of the quantum theory.

I requested, I demanded explanations. Gently, in the tone that one uses with a child, they introduced me to the existence of a certain view that was held by certain people, but, I was always told, "We must hope that it will very soon disappear." What was it? Color prejudice.

> It [colour prejudice] is nothing more than the unreasoning hatred of one race for another, the contempt of the stronger and richer peoples for those whom they consider inferior to themselves, and the bitter resentment of those who are kept in subjection and are so frequently insulted. As colour is the most obvious outward manifestation of race it has been made the criterion by which men are judged, irrespective of their social or educational attainments. The light-skinned races have come to despise all those of a darker colour, and the dark-skinned peoples will no longer accept without protest the inferior position to which they have been relegated.[2]

I had read it rightly. It was hate; I was hated, despised, detested, not by the neighbor across the street or my cousin on my mother's side, but by an entire race. I was up against something unreasoned. The psychoanalysts say that nothing is more traumatizing for the young child than his encounters with what is rational. I would personally say that for a man whose only weapon is reason there is nothing more neurotic than contact with unreason.

I felt knife blades open within me. I resolved to defend myself. As a good tactician, I intended to rationalize the world and to show the white man that he was mistaken.

In the Jew, Jean-Paul Sartre says, there is

> a sort of impassioned imperialism of reason: for he wishes not only to convince others that he is right; his goal is to persuade them that there is an absolute and unconditioned value to rationalism. He feels himself to be a missionary of the universal; against the universality of the Catholic reli-

2. Sir Alan Burns, *Colour Prejudice* (London, Allen and Unwin, 1948), p. 16.

gion, from which he is excluded, he asserts the "catholicity" of the rational, an instrument by which to attain to the truth and establish a spiritual bond among men.[3]

And, the author adds, though there may be Jews who have made intuition the basic category of their philosophy, their intuition

> has no resemblance to the Pascalian subtlety of spirit, and it is this latter—based on a thousand imperceptible perceptions—which to the Jew seems his worst enemy. As for Bergson, his philosophy offers the curious appearance of an anti-intellectualist doctrine constructed entirely by the most rational and most critical of intelligences. It is through argument that he establishes the existence of pure duration, of philosophic intuition; and that very intuition which discovers duration or life, is itself universal, since anyone may practice it, and it leads toward the universal, since its objects can be named and conceived.[4]

With enthusiasm I set to cataloguing and probing my surroundings. As times changed, one had seen the Catholic religion at first justify and then condemn slavery and prejudices. But by referring everything to the idea of the dignity of man, one had ripped prejudice to shreds. After much reluctance, the scientists had conceded that the Negro was a human being; *in vivo* and *in vitro* the Negro had been proved analogous to the white man: the same morphology, the same histology. Reason was confident of victory on every level. I put all the parts back together. But I had to change my tune.

That victory played cat and mouse; it made a fool of me. As the other put it, when I was present, it was not;

---

3. *Anti-Semite and Jew* (New York, Grove Press, 1960), pp. 112-113.

4. *Ibid.*, p. 115.

when it was there, I was no longer. In the abstract there was agreement: The Negro is a human being. That is to say, amended the less firmly convinced, that like us he has his heart on the left side. But on certain points the white man remained intractable. Under no conditions did he wish any intimacy between the races, for it is a truism that "crossings between widely different races can lower the physical and mental level. . . . Until we have a more definite knowledge of the effect of race-crossings we shall certainly do best to avoid crossings between widely different races."[5]

For my own part, I would certainly know how to react. And in one sense, if I were asked for a definition of myself, I would say that I am one who waits; I investigate my surroundings, I interpret everything in terms of what I discover, I become sensitive.

In the first chapter of the history that the others have compiled for me, the foundation of cannibalism has been made eminently plain in order that I may not lose sight of it. My chromosomes were supposed to have a few thicker or thinner genes representing cannibalism. In addition to the *sex-linked*, the scholars had now discovered the *racial-linked*.[6] What a shameful science!

But I understand this "psychological mechanism." For it is a matter of common knowledge that the mechanism is only psychological. Two centuries ago I was lost to humanity, I was a slave forever. And then came men who said that it all had gone on far too long. My tenaciousness

5. Jon Alfred Mjoen, "Harmonic and Disharmonic Race-crossings," The Second International Congress of Eugenics (1921), *Eugenics in Race and State*, vol. II, p. 60, quoted in Sir Alan Burns, *op. cit.*, p. 120.

6. In English in the original. (Translator's note.)

did the rest; I was saved from the civilizing deluge. I have gone forward.

Too late. Everything is anticipated, thought out, demonstrated, made the most of. My trembling hands take hold of nothing; the vein has been mined out. Too late! But once again I want to understand.

Since the time when someone first mourned the fact that he had arrived too late and everything had been said, a nostalgia for the past has seemed to persist. Is this that lost original paradise of which Otto Rank speaks? How many such men, apparently rooted to the womb of the world, have devoted their lives to studying the Delphic oracles or exhausted themselves in attempts to plot the wanderings of Ulysses! The pan-spiritualists seek to prove the existence of a soul in animals by using this argument: A dog lies down on the grave of his master and starves to death there. We had to wait for Janet to demonstrate that the aforesaid dog, in contrast to man, simply lacked the capacity to liquidate the past. We speak of the glory of Greece, Artaud says; but, he adds, if modern man can no longer understand the *Choephoroi* of Aeschylus, it is Aeschylus who is to blame. It is tradition to which the anti-Semites turn in order to ground the validity of their "point of view." It is tradition, it is that long historical past, it is that blood relation between Pascal and Descartes, that is invoked when the Jew is told, "There is no possibility of your finding a place in society." Not long ago, one of those good Frenchmen said in a train where I was sitting: "Just let the real French virtues keep going and the race is safe. Now more than ever, national union must be made a reality. Let's have an end of internal strife! Let's face up to the foreigners (here he turned toward my corner) no matter who they are."

It must be said in his defense that he stank of cheap wine; if he had been capable of it, he would have told me that my emancipated-slave blood could not possibly be stirred by the name of Villon or Taine.

An outrage!

The Jew and I: Since I was not satisfied to be racialized, by a lucky turn of fate I was humanized. I joined the Jew, my brother in misery.

An outrage!

At first thought it may seem strange that the anti-Semite's outlook should be related to that of the Negrophobe. It was my philosophy professor, a native of the Antilles, who recalled the fact to me one day: "Whenever you hear anyone abuse the Jews, pay attention, because he is talking about you." And I found that he was universally right—by which I meant that I was answerable in my body and in my heart for what was done to my brother. Later I realized that he meant, quite simply, an anti-Semite is inevitably anti-Negro.

You come too late, much too late. There will always be a world—a white world—between you and us. . . . The other's total inability to liquidate the past once and for all. In the face of this affective ankylosis of the white man, it is understandable that I could have made up my mind to utter my Negro cry. Little by little, putting out pseudopodia here and there, I secreted a race. And that race staggered under the burden of a basic element. What was it? *Rhythm!* Listen to our singer, Léopold Senghor:

> It is the thing that is most perceptible and least material. It is the archetype of the vital element. It is the first condition and the hallmark of Art, as breath is of life: breath, which accelerates or slows, which becomes even or agitated according to the tension in the individual, the degree and the nature of his emotion. This is rhythm in its primordial

> purity, this is rhythm in the masterpieces of Negro art, especially sculpture. It is composed of a theme—sculptural form—which is set in opposition to a sister theme, as inhalation is to exhalation, and that is repeated. It is not the kind of symmetry that gives rise to monotony; rhythm is alive, it is free. . . . This is how rhythm affects what is least intellectual in us, tyrannically, to make us penetrate to the spirituality of the object; and that character of abandon which is ours is itself rhythmic.[7]

Had I read that right? I read it again with redoubled attention. From the opposite end of the white world a magical Negro culture was hailing me. Negro sculpture! I began to flush with pride. Was this our salvation?

I had rationalized the world and the world had rejected me on the basis of color prejudice. Since no agreement was possible on the level of reason, I threw myself back toward unreason. It was up to the white man to be more irrational than I. Out of the necessities of my struggle I had chosen the method of regression, but the fact remained that it was an unfamiliar weapon; here I am at home; I am made of the irrational; I wade in the irrational. Up to the neck in the irrational. And now how my voice vibrates!

> Those who invented neither gunpowder nor the compass
> Those who never learned to conquer steam or electricity
> Those who never explored the seas or the skies
> But they know the farthest corners of the land of anguish
> Those who never knew any journey save that of abduction
> Those who learned to kneel in docility
> Those who were domesticated and Christianized
> Those who were injected with bastardy. . . .

---

7. "Ce que l'homme noir apporte," in Claude Nordey, *L'Homme de couleur* (Paris, Plon, 1939), pp. 309-310.

Yes, all those are my brothers—a "bitter brotherhood" imprisons all of us alike. Having stated the minor thesis, I went overboard after something else.

> . . . But those without whom the earth would not be
> the earth
> Tumescence all the more fruitful
> than
> the empty land
> still more the land
> Storehouse to guard and ripen all
> on earth that is most earth
> My blackness is no stone, its deafness
> hurled against the clamor of the day
> My blackness is no drop of lifeless water
> on the dead eye of the world
> My blackness is neither a tower nor a cathedral
> It thrusts into the red flesh of the sun
> It thrusts into the burning flesh of the sky
> It hollows through the dense dismay of its own
> pillar of patience.[8]

Eyah! the tom-tom chatters out the cosmic message. Only the Negro has the capacity to convey it, to decipher its meaning, its import. Astride the world, my strong heels spurring into the flanks of the world, I stare into the shoulders of the world as the celebrant stares at the midpoint between the eyes of the sacrificial victim.

> But they abandon themselves, possessed, to the essence of all things, knowing nothing of externals but possessed by the movement of all things
> uncaring to subdue but playing the play of the world
> truly the eldest sons of the world

8. Aimé Césaire, *Cahier d'un retour au pays natal* (Paris, Présence Africaine, 1956), pp. 77-78.

> open to all the breaths of the world
> meeting-place of all the winds of the world
> undrained bed of all the waters of the world
> spark of the sacred fire of the World
> flesh of the flesh of the world, throbbing with the
> very movement of the world![9]

Blood! Blood! . . . Birth! Ecstasy of becoming! Three-quarters engulfed in the confusions of the day, I feel myself redden with blood. The arteries of all the world, convulsed, torn away, uprooted, have turned toward me and fed me.

"Blood! Blood! All our blood stirred by the male heart of the sun."[10]

Sacrifice was a middle point between the creation and myself—now I went back no longer to sources but to The Source. Nevertheless, one had to distrust rhythm, earth-mother love, this mystic, carnal marriage of the group and the cosmos.

In *La vie sexuelle en Afrique noire*, a work rich in perceptions, De Pédrals implies that always in Africa, no matter what field is studied, it will have a certain magico-social structure. He adds:

> All these are the elements that one finds again on a still greater scale in the domain of secret societies. To the extent, moreover, to which persons of either sex, subjected to circumcision during adolescence, are bound under penalty of death not to reveal to the uninitiated what they have experienced, and to the extent to which initiation into a secret society always excites to acts of *sacred love*, there is good ground to conclude by viewing both male and female

9. *Ibid.*, p. 78.
10. *Ibid.*, p. 79.

circumcision and the rites that they embellish as constitutive of minor secret societies.[11]

I walk on white nails. Sheets of water threaten my soul on fire. Face to face with these rites, I am doubly alert. Black magic! Orgies, witches' sabbaths, heathen ceremonies, amulets. Coitus is an occasion to call on the gods of the clan. It is a sacred act, pure, absolute, bringing invisible forces into action. What is one to think of all these manifestations, all these initiations, all these acts? From very direction I am assaulted by the obscenity of dances and of words. Almost at my ear there is a song:

First our hearts burned hot
Now they are cold
All we think of now is Love
When we return to the village
When we see the great phallus
Ah how then we will make Love
For our parts will be dry and clean.[12]

The soil, which only a moment ago was still a tamed steed, begins to revel. Are these virgins, these nymphomaniacs? Black Magic, primitive mentality, animism, animal eroticism, it all floods over me. All of it is typical of peoples that have not kept pace with the evolution of the human race. Or, if one prefers, this is humanity at its lowest. Having reached this point, I was long reluctant to commit myself. Aggression was in the stars. I had to choose. What do I mean? I had no choice. . . .

Yes, we are—we Negroes—backward, simple, free in our behavior. That is because for us the body is not some-

---

11. De Pédrals, *La vie sexuelle en Afrique noire* (Paris, Payot), p. 83.

12. A. M. Vergiat, *Les rites secrets des primitifs de l'Oubangui* (Paris, Payot, 1951), p. 113.

thing opposed to what you call the mind. We are in the world. And long live the couple, Man and Earth! Besides, our men of letters helped me to convince you; your white civilization overlooks subtle riches and sensitivity. Listen:

> Emotive sensitivity. *Emotion is completely Negro as reason is Greek.*[13] Water rippled by every breeze? Unsheltered soul blown by every wind, whose fruit often drops before it is ripe? Yes, in one way, the Negro today is richer *in gifts than in works.*[14] But the tree thrusts its roots into the earth. The river runs deep, carrying precious seeds. And, the Afro-American poet, Langston Hughes, says:
>
> I have known rivers
> ancient dark rivers
> my soul has grown deep
> like the deep rivers.
>
> The very nature of the Negro's emotion, of his sensitivity, furthermore, explains his attitude toward the object perceived with such basic intensity. It is an abandon that becomes need, an active state of communion, indeed of identification, however negligible the action—I almost said the personality—of the object. A rhythmic attitude: The adjective should be kept in mind.[15]

So here we have the Negro rehabilitated, "standing before the bar," ruling the world with his intuition, the Negro recognized, set on his feet again, sought after, taken up, and he is a Negro—no, he is not a Negro but the Negro, exciting the fecund antennae of the world, placed in the foreground of the world, raining his poetic power on the world, "open to all the breaths of the world." I embrace the world! I am the world! The white man has

13. My italics—F.F.
14. My italics—F.F.
15. Léopold Senghor, "Ce que l'homme noir apporte," in Nordey, *op. cit.*, p. 205.

never understood this magic substitution. The white man wants the world; he wants it for himself alone. He finds himself predestined master of this world. He enslaves it. An acquisitive relation is established between the world and him. But there exist other values that fit only my forms. Like a magician, I robbed the white man of "a certain world," forever after lost to him and his. When that happened, the white man must have been rocked backward by a force that he could not identify, so little used as he is to such reactions. Somewhere beyond the objective world of farms and banana trees and rubber trees, I had subtly brought the real world into being. The essence of the world was my fortune. Between the world and me a relation of coexistence was established. I had discovered the primeval One. My "speaking hands" tore at the hysterical throat of the world. The white man had the anguished feeling that I was escaping from him and that I was taking something with me. He went through my pockets. He thrust probes into the least circumvolution of my brain. Everywhere he found only the obvious. So it was obvious that I had a secret. I was interrogated; turning away with an air of mystery, I murmured:

> Tokowaly, uncle, do you remember the nights gone by
> When my head weighed heavy on the back of your patience
> or
> Holding my hand your hand led me by shadows and signs
> The fields are flowers of glowworms, stars hang on the bushes, on the trees
> Silence is everywhere
> Only the scents of the jungle hum, swarms of reddish bees that overwhelm the crickets' shrill sounds,
> And covered tom-tom, breathing in the distance of the night.
> You, Tokowaly, you listen to what cannot be heard, and

you explain to me what the ancestors are saying in the
liquid calm of the constellations,
The bull, the scorpion, the leopard, the elephant,
and the fish we know,
And the white pomp of the Spirits in the heavenly shell
that has no end,
But now comes the radiance of the goddess Moon
and the veils of the shadows fall.
Night of Africa, my black night, mystical and bright, black
and shining.[16]

I made myself the poet of the world. The white man had found a poetry in which there was nothing poetic. The soul of the white man was corrupted, and, as I was told by a friend who was a teacher in the United States, "The presence of the Negroes beside the whites is in a way an insurance policy on humanness. When the whites feel that they have become too mechanized, they turn to the men of color and ask them for a little human sustenance." At last I had been recognized, I was no longer a zero.

I had soon to change my tune. Only momentarily at a loss, the white man explained to me that, genetically, I represented a stage of development: "Your properties have been exhausted by us. We have had earth mystics such as you will never approach. Study our history and you will see how far this fusion has gone." Then I had the feeling that I was repeating a cycle. My originality had been torn out of me. I wept a long time, and then I began to live again. But I was haunted by a galaxy of erosive stereotypes: the Negro's *sui generis* odor . . . the Negro's *sui generis* good nature . . . the Negro's *sui generis* gullibility. . . .

16. Léopold Senghor, *Chants d'ombre* (Paris, Editions du Seuil, 1945).

I had tried to flee myself through my kind, but the whites had thrown themselves on me and hamstrung me. I tested the limits of my essence; beyond all doubt there was not much of it left. It was here that I made my most remarkable discovery. Properly speaking, this discovery was a rediscovery.

I rummaged frenetically through all the antiquity of the black man. What I found there took away my breath. In his book *L'abolition de l'esclavage* Schoelcher presented us with compelling arguments. Since then, Frobenius, Westermann, Delafosse—all of them white—had joined the chorus: Ségou, Djenné, cities of more than a hundred thousand people; accounts of learned blacks (doctors of theology who went to Mecca to interpret the Koran). All of that, exhumed from the past, spread with its insides out, made it possible for me to find a valid historic place. The white man was wrong, I was not a primitive, not even a half-man, I belonged to a race that had already been working in gold and silver two thousand years ago. And too there was something else, something else that the white man could not understand. Listen:

> What sort of men were these, then, who had been torn away from their families, their countries, their religions, with a savagery unparalleled in history?
>
> Gentle men, polite, considerate, unquestionably superior to those who tortured them—that collection of adventurers who slashed and violated and spat on Africa to make the stripping of her the easier.
>
> The men they took away knew how to build houses, govern empires, erect cities, cultivate fields, mine for metals, weave cotton, forge steel.
>
> Their religion had its own beauty, based on mystical connections with the founder of the city. Their customs were pleasing, built on unity, kindness, respect for age.

> No coercion, only mutual assistance, the joy of living, a free acceptance of discipline.
>
> Order—Earnestness—Poetry and Freedom.
>
> From the untroubled private citizen to the almost fabulous leader there was an unbroken chain of understanding and trust. No science? Indeed yes; but also, to protect them from fear, they possessed great myths in which the most subtle observation and the most daring imagination were balanced and blended. No art? They had their magnificent sculpture, in which human feeling erupted so unrestrained yet always followed the obsessive laws of rhythm in its organization of the major elements of a material called upon to capture, in order to redistribute, the most secret forces of the universe. . . .[17]
>
> Monuments in the very heart of Africa? Schools? Hospitals? Not a single good burgher of the twentieth century, no Durand, no Smith, no Brown even suspects that such things existed in Africa before the Europeans came. . . .
>
> But Schoelcher reminds us of their presence, discovered by Caillé, Mollien, the Cander brothers. And, though he nowhere reminds us that when the Portuguese landed on the banks of the Congo in 1498, they found a rich and flourishing state there and that the courtiers of Ambas were dressed in robes of silk and brocade, at least he knows that Africa had brought itself up to a juridical concept of the state, and he is aware, living in the very flood of imperialism, that European civilization, after all, is only one more civilization among many—and not the most merciful.[18]

I put the white man back into his place; growing bolder, I jostled him and told him point-blank, "Get used to me, I am not getting used to anyone." I shouted my laughter to the stars. The white man, I could see, was

17. Aimé Césaire, Introduction to Victor Schoelcher, *Esclavage et colonisation* (Paris, Presses Universitaires de France, 1948), p. 7.
18. *Ibid.*, p. 8.

resentful. His reaction time lagged interminably. . . . I had won. I was jubilant.

"Lay aside your history, your investigations of the past, and try to feel yourself into our rhythm. In a society such as ours, industrialized to the highest degree, dominated by scientism, there is no longer room for your sensitivity. One must be tough if one is to be allowed to live. What matters now is no longer playing the game of the world but subjugating it with integers and atoms. Oh, certainly, I will be told, now and then when we are worn out by our lives in big buildings, we will turn to you as we do to our children—to the innocent, the ingenuous, the spontaneous. We will turn to you as to the childhood of the world. You are so real in your life—so funny, that is. Let us run away for a little while from our ritualized, polite civilization and let us relax, bend to those heads, those adorably expressive faces. In a way, you reconcile us with ourselves."

Thus my unreason was countered with reason, my reason with "real reason." Every hand was a losing hand for me. I analyzed my heredity. I made a complete audit of my ailment. I wanted to be typically Negro—it was no longer possible. I wanted to be white—that was a joke. And, when I tried, on the level of ideas and intellectual activity, to reclaim my negritude, it was snatched away from me. Proof was presented that my effort was only a term in the dialectic:

> But there is something more important: The Negro, as we have said, creates an anti-racist racism for himself. In no sense does he wish to rule the world: He seeks the abolition of all ethnic privileges, wherever they come from; he asserts his solidarity with the oppressed of all colors. At once the subjective, existential, ethnic idea of *negritude* "passes," as Hegel puts it, into the objective, positive, exact idea of

> *proletariat*. "For Césaire," Senghor says, "the white man is the symbol of capital as the Negro is that of labor. . . . Beyond the black-skinned men of his race it is the battle of the world proletariat that is his song."
>
> That is easy to say, but less easy to think out. And undoubtedly it is no coincidence that the most ardent poets of negritude are at the same time militant Marxists.
>
> But that does not prevent the idea of race from mingling with that of class: The first is concrete and particular, the second is universal and abstract; the one stems from what Jaspers calls understanding and the other from intellection; the first is the result of a psychobiological syncretism and the second is a methodical construction based on experience. In fact, negritude appears as the minor term of a dialectical progression: The theoretical and practical assertion of the supremacy of the white man is its thesis; the position of negritude as an antithetical value is the moment of negativity. But this negative moment is insufficient by itself, and the Negroes who employ it know this very well; they know that it is intended to prepare the synthesis or realization of the human in a society without races. Thus negritude is the root of its own destruction, it is a transition and not a conclusion, a means and not an ultimate end.[19]

When I read that page, I felt that I had been robbed of my last chance. I said to my friends, "The generation of the younger black poets has just suffered a blow that can never be forgiven." Help had been sought from a friend of the colored peoples, and that friend had found no better response than to point out the relativity of what they were doing. For once, that born Hegelian had forgotten that consciousness has to lose itself in the night of the absolute, the only condition to attain to conscious-

19. Jean-Paul Sartre, *Orphée Noir*, preface to *Anthologie de la nouvelle poésie nègre et malgache* (Paris, Presses Universitaires de France, 1948), pp. xl ff.

ness of self. In opposition to rationalism, he summoned up the negative side, but he forgot that this negativity draws its worth from an almost substantive absoluteness. A consciousness committed to experience is ignorant, has to be ignorant, of the essences and the determinations of its being.

Orphée Noir is a date in the intellectualization of the *experience* of being black. And Sartre's mistake was not only to seek the source of the source but in a certain sense to block that source:

> Will the source of Poetry be dried up? Or will the great black flood, in spite of everything, color the sea into which it pours itself? It does not matter: Every age has its own poetry; in every age the circumstances of history choose a nation, a race, a class to take up the torch by creating situations that can be expressed or transcended only through Poetry; sometimes the poetic impulse coincides with the revolutionary impulse, and sometimes they take different courses. Today let us hail the turn of history that will make it possible for the black men to utter "the great Negro cry with a force that will shake the pillars of the world" (Césaire).[20]

And so it is not I who make a meaning for myself, but it is the meaning that was already there, pre-existing, waiting for me. It is not out of my bad nigger's misery, my bad nigger's teeth, my bad nigger's hunger that I will shape a torch with which to burn down the woıld, but it is the torch that was already there, waiting for that turn of history.

In terms of consciousness, the black consciousness is held out as an absolute density, as filled with itself, a stage preceding any invasion, any abolition of the ego by

---

20. *Ibid.*, p. xliv.

desire. Jean-Paul Sartre, in this work, has destroyed black zeal. In opposition to historical becoming, there had always been the unforeseeable. I needed to lose myself completely in negritude. One day, perhaps, in the depths of that unhappy romanticism. . . .

In any case I *needed* not to know. This struggle, this new decline had to take on an aspect of completeness. Nothing is more unwelcome than the commonplace: "You'll change, my boy; I was like that too when I was young . . . you'll see, it will all pass."

The dialectic that brings necessity into the foundation of my freedom drives me out of myself. It shatters my unreflected position. Still in terms of consciousness, black consciousness is immanent in its own eyes. I am not a potentiality of something, I am wholly what I am. I do not have to look for the universal. No probability has any place inside me. My Negro consciousness does not hold itself out as a lack. It *is*. It is its own follower.

But, I will be told, your statements show a misreading of the processes of history. Listen then:

> Africa I have kept your memory Africa
> you are inside me
> Like the splinter in the wound
> like a guardian fetish in the center of the village
> make me the stone in your sling
> make my mouth the lips of your wound
> make my knees the broken pillars of your abasement
> AND YET
> I want to be of your race alone
> workers peasants of all lands . . .
> . . . white worker in Detroit black peon in Alabama
> uncountable nation in capitalist slavery
> destiny ranges us shoulder to shoulder
> repudiating the ancient maledictions of blood taboos

we roll away the ruins of our solitudes
If the flood is a frontier
we will strip the gully of its endless
covering flow
If the Sierra is a frontier
we will smash the jaws of the volcanoes
upholding the Cordilleras
and the plain will be the parade ground of the dawn
where we regroup our forces sundered
by the deceits of our masters
As the contradiction among the features
creates the harmony of the face
we proclaim the oneness of the suffering
and the revolt
of all the peoples on all the face of the earth
and we mix the mortar of the age of brotherhood
out of the dust of idols.[21]

Exactly, we will reply, Negro experience is not a whole, for there is not merely *one* Negro, there are *Negroes.* What a difference, for instance, in this other poem:

The white man killed my father
Because my father was proud
The white man raped my mother
Because my mother was beautiful
The white man wore out my brother in the hot sun
of the roads
Because my brother was strong
Then the white man came to me
His hands red with blood
Spat his contempt into my black face
Out of his tyrant's voice:
"Hey boy, a basin, a towel, water."[22]

---

21. Jacques Roumain, "Bois-d'Ebène," Prelude, in *Anthologie de la nouvelle poésie nègre et malgache*, p. 113.
22. David Diop, "Le temps du martyre," in *ibid.*, p. 174.

Or this other one:

> My brother with teeth that glisten at the compliments
> of hypocrites
> My brother with gold-rimmed spectacles
> Over eyes that turn blue at the sound of the Master's
> voice
> My poor brother in dinner jacket with its silk lapels
> Clucking and whispering and strutting through the
> drawing rooms of Condescension
> How pathetic you are
> The sun of your native country is nothing more now
> than a shadow
> On your composed civilized face
> And your grandmother's hut
> Brings blushes into cheeks made white by years of
> abasement and *Mea culpa*
> But when regurgitating the flood of lofty empty words
> Like the load that presses on your shoulders
> You walk again on the rough red earth of Africa
> These words of anguish will state the rhythm of your
> uneasy gait
> I feel so alone, so alone here![23]

From time to time one would like to stop. To state reality is a wearing task. But, when one has taken it into one's head to try to express existence, one runs the risk of finding only the nonexistent. What is certain is that, at the very moment when I was trying to grasp my own being, Sartre, who remained The Other, gave me a name and thus shattered my last illusion. While I was saying to him:

> "My negritude is neither a tower nor a cathedral,
> it thrusts into the red flesh of the sun,
> it thrusts into the burning flesh of the sky,

23. David Diop, "Le Renégat."

it hollows through the dense dismay of its own pillar
of patience . . ."

while I was shouting that, in the paroxysm of my being and my fury, he was reminding me that my blackness was only a minor term. In all truth, in all truth I tell you, my shoulders slipped out of the framework of the world, my feet could no longer feel the touch of the ground. Without a Negro past, without a Negro future, it was impossible for me to live my Negrohood. Not yet white, no longer wholly black, I was damned. Jean-Paul Sartre had forgotten that the Negro suffers in his body quite differently from the white man.[24] Between the white man and me the connection was irrevocably one of transcendence.[25]

But the constancy of my love had been forgotten. I defined myself as an absolute intensity of beginning. So I took up my negritude, and with tears in my eyes I put its machinery together again. What had been broken to pieces was rebuilt, reconstructed by the intuitive lianas of my hands.

My cry grew more violent: I am a Negro, I am a Negro, I am a Negro. . . .

And there was my poor brother—living out his neurosis to the extreme and finding himself paralyzed:

THE NEGRO: I can't, ma'am.
LIZZIE: Why not?

---

24. Though Sartre's speculations on the existence of The Other may be correct (to the extent, we must remember, to which *Being and Nothingness* describes an alienated consciousness), their application to a black consciousness proves fallacious. That is because the white man is not only The Other but also the master, whether real or imaginary.

25. In the sense in which the word is used by Jean Wahl in *Existence humaine et transcendance* (Neuchâtel, La Baconnière, 1944).

THE NEGRO: I can't shoot white folks.
LIZZIE: Really! That would bother them, wouldn't it?
THE NEGRO: They're white folks, ma'am.
LIZZIE: So what? Maybe they got a right to bleed you like a pig just because they're white?
THE NEGRO: But they're white folks.

A feeling of inferiority? No, a feeling of nonexistence. Sin is Negro as virtue is white. All those white men in a group, guns in their hands, cannot be wrong. I am guilty. I do not know of what, but I know that I am no good.

THE NEGRO: That's how it goes, ma'am. That's how it always goes with white folks.
LIZZIE: You too? You feel guilty?
THE NEGRO: Yes, ma'am.[26]

It is Bigger Thomas—he is afraid, he is terribly afraid. He is afraid, but of what is he afraid? Of himself. No one knows yet who he is, but he knows that fear will fill the world when the world finds out. And when the world knows, the world always expects something of the Negro. He is afraid lest the world know, he is afraid of the fear that the world would feel if the world knew. Like that old woman on her knees who begged me to tie her to her bed:

"I just know, Doctor: Any minute that thing will take hold of me."

"What thing?"

"The wanting to kill myself. Tie me down, I'm afraid."

In the end, Bigger Thomas acts. To put an end to his tension, he acts, he responds to the world's anticipation.[27]

---

26. Jean-Paul Sartre, *The Respectful Prostitute*, in *Three Plays* (New York, Knopf, 1949), pp. 189, 191. Originally, *La Putain respectueuse* (Paris, Gallimard, 1947). See also *Home of the Brave*, a film by Mark Robson.

27. Richard Wright, *Native Son* (New York, Harper, 1940).

So it is with the character in *If He Hollers Let Him Go*[28] —who does precisely what he did not want to do. That big blonde who was always in his way, weak, sensual, offered, open, fearing (desiring) rape, became his mistress in the end.

The Negro is a toy in the white man's hands; so, in order to shatter the hellish cycle, he explodes. I cannot go to a film without seeing myself. I wait for me. In the interval, just before the film starts, I wait for me. The people in the theater are watching me, examining me, waiting for me. A Negro groom is going to appear. My heart makes my head swim.

The crippled veteran of the Pacific war says to my brother, "Resign yourself to your color the way I got used to my stump; we're both victims."[29]

Nevertheless with all my strength I refuse to accept that amputation. I feel in myself a soul as immense as the world, truly a soul as deep as the deepest of rivers, my chest has the power to expand without limit. I am a master and I am advised to adopt the humility of the cripple. Yesterday, awakening to the world, I saw the sky turn upon itself utterly and wholly. I wanted to rise, but the disemboweled silence fell back upon me, its wings paralyzed. Without responsibility, straddling Nothingness and Infinity, I began to weep.

---

28. By Chester Himes (Garden City, Doubleday, 1945).
29. *Home of the Brave*.

Chapter Six

THE NEGRO AND PSYCHOPATHOLOGY

Psychoanalytic schools have studied the neurotic reactions that arise among certain groups, in certain areas of civilization. In response to the requirements of dialectic, one should investigate the extent to which the conclusions of Freud or of Adler can be applied to the effort to understand the man of color's view of the world.

It can never be sufficiently emphasized that psychoanalysis sets as its task the understanding of given behavior patterns—within the specific group represented by the family. When the problem is a neurosis experienced by an adult, the analyst's task is to uncover in the new psychic structure an analogy with certain infantile elements, a repetition, a duplication of conflicts that owe their origin to the essence of the family constellation. In every case the analyst clings to the concept of the family as a "psychic circumstance and object."[1]

Here, however, the evidence is going to be particularly complicated. In Europe the family represents in effect a certain fashion in which the world presents itself to the child. There are close connections between the structure of the family and the structure of the nation. Militariza-

1. Jacques Lacan, "Le complèxe, facteur concret de la psychologie familiale," *Encyclopédie française*, 8-40, 5.

tion and the centralization of authority in a country automatically entail a resurgence of the authority of the father. In Europe and in every country characterized as civilized or civilizing, the family is a miniature of the nation. As the child emerges from the shadow of his parents, he finds himself once more among the same laws, the same principles, the same values. A normal child that has grown up in a normal family will be a normal man.[2] There is no disproportion between the life of the family and the life of the nation. Conversely, when one examines a closed society—that is, a society that has been protected from the flood of civilization—one encounters the same structures as those just described. Father Trilles' *L'âme du Pygmée d'Afrique,* for instance, convinces us of that; although with every word one is aware of the need to Christianize the savage Negro soul, the book's description of the whole culture—the conditions of worship, the persistence of rites, the survival of myths—has nothing of the artificial impression given by *La philosophie bantoue.*

In both cases the characteristics of the family are projected onto the social environment. It is true that the children of pickpockets or burglars, accustomed to a certain system of clan law, would be surprised to find that the rest of the world behaved differently, but a new kind of

---

2. I should like to think that I am not going to be brought to trial for this sentence. Skeptics always have a fine time asking, "What do you mean by *normal*?" For the moment, it is beyond the scope of this book to answer the question. In order to pacify the more insistent, let me refer them to the extremely instructive work by Georges Canguilhem, *Essai sur quelques problèmes concernant le normal et le pathologique* (Paris, Société d'Editions, 1950), even though its sole orientation is biological. And let me add only that in the psychological sphere the abnormal man is he who demands, who appeals, who begs.

training—except in instances of perversion or arrested development (Heuyer)[3]—should be able to direct them into a moralization, a socialization of outlook.

It is apparent in all such cases that the sickness lies in the family environment.

> For the individual the authority of the state is a reproduction of the authority of the family by which he was shaped in his childhood. Ultimately the individual assimilates all the authorities that he meets to the authority of the parents: He perceives the present in terms of the past. Like all other human conduct, behavior toward authority is something learned. And it is learned in the heart of a family that can be described, from the psychological point of view, by the form of organization peculiar to it—that is, by the way in which its authority is distributed and exercised.[4]

But—and this is a most important point—we observe the opposite in the man of color. A normal Negro child, having grown up within a normal family, will become abnormal on the slightest contact with the white world. This statement may not be immediately understandable. Therefore let us proceed by going backward. Paying tribute to Dr. Breuer, Freud wrote:

> In almost every case, we could see that the symptoms were, so to speak, like residues of emotional experiences, to which

3. Although even this reservation is open to argument. See for example the question put by Mlle. Juliette Boutonnier: "Might not perversion be an extreme arrest in affect development, furthered, if not produced, by the conditions under which the child has lived, at least as much as by the congenital tendencies that are obviously factors in it but that probably are not alone responsible?" (*Revue Française de Psychanalyse*, No. 3, 1949, pp. 403-404.)

4. Joachim Marcus, "Structure familiale et comportements politiques," L'autorité dans la famille et dans l'État, *Revue Française de Psychanalyse*, April-June, 1949.

> for this reason we later gave the name of psychic traumas. Their individual characters were linked to the traumatic scenes that had provoked them. According to the classic terminology, the symptoms were determined by "scenes" of which they were the mnemic residues, and it was no longer necessary to regard them as arbitrary and enigmatic effects of the neurosis. In contrast, however, to what was expected, it was not always a single event that was the cause of the symptom; most often, on the contrary, it arose out of multiple traumas, frequently analogous and repeated. As a result, it became necessary to reproduce chronologically this whole series of pathogenic memories, but in reverse order: the latest at the beginning and the earliest at the end; it was impossible to make one's way back to the first trauma, which is often the most forceful, if one skipped any of its successors.

It could not be stated more positively; every neurosis has its origins in specific *Erlebnisse*. Later Freud added:

> This trauma, it is true, has been quite expelled from the consciousness and the memory of the patient and as a result he has apparently been saved from a great mass of suffering, but the repressed desire continues to exist in the unconscious; it is on watch constantly for an opportunity to make itself known and it soon comes back into consciousness, but in a disguise that makes it impossible to recognize; in other words, the repressed thought is replaced in consciousness by another that acts as its surrogate, its *Ersatz*, and that soon surrounds itself with all those feelings of morbidity that had been supposedly averted by the repression.

These *Erlebnisse* are repressed in the unconscious.

What do we see in the case of the black man? Unless we make use of that frightening postulate—which so destroys our balance—offered by Jung, the *collective un-*

conscious, we can understand absolutely nothing. A drama is enacted every day in colonized countries. How is one to explain, for example, that a Negro who has passed his baccalaureate and has gone to the Sorbonne to study to become a teacher of philosophy is already on guard before any conflictual elements have coalesced round him? René Ménil accounted for this reaction in Hegelian terms. In his view it was "the consequence of the replacement of the repressed [African] spirit in the consciousness of the slave by an authority symbol representing the Master, a symbol implanted in the subsoil of the collective group and charged with maintaining order in it as a garrison controls a conquered city."[5]

We shall see in our section on Hegel that René Ménil has made no misjudgment. Meanwhile we have the right to put a question to ourselves: How is the persistence of this reaction in the twentieth century to be explained when in other ways there is complete identification with the white man? Very often the Negro who becomes abnormal has never had any relations with whites. Has some remote experience been repressed in his unconscious? Did the little black child see his father beaten or lynched by a white man? Has there been a real traumatism? To all of this we have to answer *no*. Well, then?

If we want to answer correctly, we have to fall back on the idea of *collective catharsis*. In every society, in every collectivity, exists—must exist—a channel, an outlet through which the forces accumulated in the form of aggression can be released. This is the purpose of games in children's institutions, of psychodramas in group therapy, and, in a more general way, of illustrated magazines for children

5. A quotation borrowed from Michel Leiris, "Martinique, Guadeloupe, Haiti," *Les Temps Modernes*, February, 1950, p. 1346.

—each type of society, of course, requiring its own specific kind of catharsis. The Tarzan stories, the sagas of twelve-year-old explorers, the adventures of Mickey Mouse, and all those "comic books" serve actually as a release for collective aggression. The magazines are put together by white men for little white men. This is the heart of the problem. In the Antilles—and there is every reason to think that the situation is the same in the other colonies—these same magazines are devoured by the local children. In the magazines the Wolf, the Devil, the Evil Spirit, the Bad Man, the Savage are always symbolized by Negroes or Indians; since there is always identification with the victor, the little Negro, quite as easily as the little white boy, becomes an explorer, an adventurer, a missionary "who faces the danger of being eaten by the wicked Negroes." I shall be told that this is hardly important; but only because those who say it have not given much thought to the role of such magazines. Here is what G. Legman thinks of them:

> With very rare exceptions, every American child who was six years old in 1938 had therefore assimilated at the very least 18,000 scenes of ferocious tortures and bloody violence. . . . Except the Boers, the Americans are the only modern nation that within living memory has completely driven the autochthonous population off the soil that it had occupied.[6] America alone, then, could have had an uneasy national conscience to lull by creating the myth of the "Bad Injun,"[7] in order later to be able to bring back the historic figure of the Noble Redskin vainly defending his lands against invaders armed with rifles and Bibles; the punishment that we deserve can be averted only by denying re-

6. In this connection, it is worth noting that the Caribs experienced the same fate at the hands of French and Spanish explorers.

7. In English in the original. (Translator's note.)

> sponsibility for the wrong and throwing the blame on the victim; by proving—at least to our own satisfaction—that by striking the first and only blow we were acting solely on the legitimate ground of defense. . . . [Anticipating the repercussions of these magazines on American culture, Legman went on:] There is still no answer to the question whether this maniacal fixation on violence and death is the substitute for a forbidden sexuality or whether it does not rather serve the purpose of channeling, along a line left open by sexual censorship, both the child's and the adult's desire for aggression against the economic and social structure which, though with their entire consent, perverts them. In both cases the root of the perversion, whether it be of a sexual or of an economic character, is of the essence; that is why, as long as we remain incapable of attacking these fundamental repressions, every attack aimed at such simple escape devices as comic books will remain futile.[8]

The black schoolboy in the Antilles, who in his lessons is forever talking about "our ancestors, the Gauls,"[9] identifies himself with the explorer, the bringer of civilization, the white man who carries truth to savages—an all-white truth. There is identification—that is, the young Negro subjectively adopts a white man's attitude. He invests the hero, who is white, with all his own aggression—at that age closely linked to sacrificial dedication, a sacrificial dedication permeated with sadism. An eight-year-old child who offers a gift, even to an adult, cannot endure

8. G. Legman, "Psychopathologie des Comics," French translation by H. Robillot, *Les Temps Modernes*, May, 1949, pp. 919 ff.

9. One always sees a smile when one reports this aspect of education in Martinique. The smile comes because the comicality of the thing is obvious, but no one pursues it to its later consequences. Yet these are the important aspects, because three or four such phrases are the basis on which the young Antillean works out his view of the world.

a refusal. Little by little, one can observe in the young Antillean the formation and crystallization of an attitude and a way of thinking and seeing that are essentially white. When in school he has to read stories of savages told by white men, he always thinks of the Senegalese. As a schoolboy, I had many occasions to spend whole hours talking about the supposed customs of the savage Senegalese. In what was said there was a lack of awareness that was at the very least paradoxical. Because the Antillean does not think of himself as a black man; he thinks of himself as an Antillean. The Negro lives in Africa. Subjectively, intellectually, the Antillean conducts himself like a white man. But he is a Negro. That he will learn once he goes to Europe; and when he hears Negroes mentioned he will recognize that the word includes himself as well as the Senegalese. What are we to conclude on this matter?

To impose the same "Evil Spirits" on the white man and on the black man is a major error in education. If one is willing to understand the "Evil Spirit" in the sense of an attempt to personify the *id*, the point of view will be understood. If we are utterly honest, we must say that children's counting-out rhymes are subject to the same criticism. It will have already been noticed that I should like nothing more nor less than the establishment of children's magazines especially for Negroes, the creation of songs for Negro children, and, ultimately, the publication of history texts especially for them, at least through the grammar-school grades. For, until there is evidence to the contrary, I believe that if there is a traumatism it occurs during those years. The young Antillean is a Frenchman called on at all times to live with white compatriots. One forgets this rather too often.

The white family is the agent of a certain system. The

society is indeed the sum of all the families in it. The family is an institution that prefigures a broader institution: the social or the national group. Both turn on the same axes. The white family is the workshop in which one is shaped and trained for life in society. "The family structure is internalized in the superego," Marcus says, "and projected into political [though I would say social] behavior."

As long as he remains among his own people, the little black follows very nearly the same course as the little white. But if he goes to Europe, he will have to reappraise his lot. For the Negro in France, which is his country, will feel different from other people. One can hear the glib remark: The Negro makes himself inferior. But the truth is that he is made inferior. The young Antillean is a Frenchman called upon constantly to live with white compatriots. Now, the Antillean family has for all practical purposes no connection with the national—that is, the French, or European—structure. The Antillean has therefore to choose between his family and European society; in other words, the individual who *climbs up* into society —white and civilized—tends to reject his family—black and savage—on the plane of imagination, in accord with the childhood *Erlebnisse* that we discussed earlier. In this case the schema of Marcus becomes

Family ← Individual → Society

and the family structure is cast back into the *id*.

The Negro recognizes the unreality of many of the beliefs that he has adopted with reference to the subjective attitude of the white man. When he does, his real apprenticeship begins. And reality proves to be extremely resistant. But, it will be objected, you are merely describing a universal phenomenon, the criterion of maturity being in fact adaptation to society. My answer is that such a criticism goes off in the wrong direction, for I have just shown that for the Negro there is a myth to be faced. A solidly established myth. The Negro is unaware of it as long as his existence is limited to his own environment; but the first encounter with a white man oppresses him with the whole weight of his blackness.[10]

Then there is the unconscious. Since the racial drama is played out in the open, the black man has no time to "make it unconscious." The white man, on the other hand, succeeds in doing so to a certain extent, because a new element appears: guilt. The Negro's inferiority or superiority complex or his feeling of equality is *conscious*. These feelings forever chill him. They make his drama. In him there is none of the affective amnesia characteristic of the typical neurotic.

Whenever I have read a psychoanalytic work, discussed problems with my professors, or talked with European patients, I have been struck by the disparity between the corresponding schemas and the reality that the Negro presents. It has led me progressively to the conclusion

---

10. In this connection it is worth remembering what Sartre said:

> Some children, at the age of five or six, have already had fights with schoolmates who call them "Yids." Others may remain in ignorance for a long time. A young Jewish girl in a family I am acquainted with did not even know the meaning of the word *Jew* until she was fifteen. During the Occupation there was a Jewish doctor who lived shut up in his home at Fontainebleau and raised his children without saying a word to them of their origin. But however it comes about, some day they must learn the truth: sometimes from the smiles of those around them, sometimes from rumor or insult. The later the discovery, the more violent the shock. Suddenly they perceive that others know something about them that they do not know, that people apply to them an ugly and upsetting term that is not used in their own families. (*Anti-Semite and Jew*, p. 75.)

that there is a dialectical substitution when one goes from the psychology of the white man to that of the black.

The earliest values, which Charles Odier describes,[11] are different in the white man and in the black man. The drive toward socialization does not stem from the same motivations. In cold actuality, we change worlds. A close study should be divided into two parts:

1. a psychoanalytic interpretation of the life experience of the black man;
2. a psychoanalytic interpretation of the Negro myth.

But reality, which is our only recourse, prevents such procedures. The facts are much more complicated. What are they?

The Negro is a phobogenic object, a stimulus to anxiety. From the patient treated by Sérieux and Capgras[12] to the girl who confides to me that to go to bed with a Negro would be terrifying to her, one discovers all the stages of what I shall call the Negro-phobogenesis. There has been much talk of psychoanalysis in connection with the Negro. Distrusting the ways in which it might be applied,[13] I have preferred to call this chapter "The Negro and Psychopathology," well aware that Freud and Adler and even the cosmic Jung did not think of the Negro in all their investigations. And they were quite right not to have. It is too often forgotten that neurosis is not a basic element of human reality. Like it or not, the Oedipus

11. *Les deux sources consciente et inconsciente de la vie morale* (Neuchâtel, La Baconnière, 1943).

12. *Les folies raisonnantes,* cited by A. Hesnard, *L'univers morbide de la faute* (Paris, Presses Universitaires de France, 1949), p. 97.

13. I am thinking here particularly of the United States. See, for example, *Home of the Brave.*

complex is far from coming into being among Negroes. It might be argued, as Malinowski contends, that the matriarchal structure is the only reason for its absence. But, putting aside the question whether the ethnologists are not so imbued with the complexes of their own civilization that they are compelled to try to find them duplicated in the peoples they study, it would be relatively easy for me to show that in the French Antilles 97 per cent of the families cannot produce one Oedipal neurosis. This incapacity is one on which we heartily congratulate ourselves.[14]

With the exception of a few misfits within the closed environment, we can say that every neurosis, every abnormal manifestation, every affective erethism in an Antillean is the product of his cultural situation. In other words, there is a constellation of postulates, a series of propositions that slowly and subtly—with the help of books, newspapers, schools and their texts, advertisements, films, radio—work their way into one's mind and shape one's view of the world of the group to which one belongs.[15] In the Antilles that view of the world is white

14. On this point psychoanalysts will be reluctant to share my view. Dr. Lacan, for instance, talks of the "abundance" of the Oedipus complex. But even if the young boy has to kill his father, it is still necessary for the father to accept being killed. I am reminded of what Hegel said: "The cradle of the child is the tomb of the parents"; and of Nicolas Calas' *Foyer d'incendie* and of Jean Lacroix' *Force et faiblesses de la famille*. The collapse of moral values in France after the war was perhaps the result of the defeat of that moral being which the nation represented. We know what such traumatisms on the family level may produce.

15. I recommend the following experiment to those who are unconvinced: Attend showings of a Tarzan film in the Antilles and in Europe. In the Antilles, the young Negro identifies himself *de facto* with Tarzan against the Negroes. This is much more difficult

because no black voice exists. The folklore of Martinique is meager, and few children in Fort-de-France know the stories of "Compè Lapin," twin brother of the Br'er Rabbit of Louisiana's Uncle Remus. A European familiar with the current trends of Negro poetry, for example, would be amazed to learn that as late as 1940 no Antillean found it possible to think of himself as a Negro. It was only with the appearance of Aimé Césaire that the acceptance of negritude and the statement of its claims began to be perceptible. The most concrete proof of this, furthermore, is that feeling which pervades each new generation of students arriving in Paris: It takes them several weeks to recognize that contact with Europe compels them to face a certain number of problems that until their arrival had never touched them. And yet these problems were by no means invisible.[16]

Whenever I had a discussion with my professors or talked with European patients, I became aware of the differences that might prevail between the two worlds.

---

for him in a European theater, for the rest of the audience, which is white, automatically identifies him with the savages on the screen. It is a conclusive experience. The Negro learns that one is not black without problems. A documentary film on Africa produces similar reactions when it is shown in a French city and in Fort-de-France. I will go farther and say that Bushmen and Zulus arouse even more laughter among the young Antilleans. It would be interesting to show how in this instance the reactional exaggeration betrays a hint of recognition. In France a Negro who sees this documentary is virtually petrified. There he has no more hope of flight: He is at once Antillean, Bushman, and Zulu.

16. More especially, they become aware that the line of self-esteem that they had chosen should be inverted. We have seen in fact that the Antillean who goes to France pictures this journey as the final stage of his personality. Quite literally I can say without any risk of error that the Antillean who goes to France in order to convince himself that he is white will find his real face there.

Talking recently to a physician who had always practiced in Fort-de-France, I told him what conclusions I had arrived at; he went farther, saying that they were valid not only in psychopathology but also in general medicine. "In the same way," he added, "you never encounter a case of pure typhoid such as you studied in the textbooks; there is always a more or less manifest complication of malaria." It would be interesting to study, for example, a case of schizophrenia as experienced by a Negro—if indeed that kind of malady were to be found there.

What am I getting at? Quite simply this: When the Negro makes contact with the white world, a certain sensitizing action takes place. If his psychic structure is weak, one observes a collapse of the ego. The black man stops behaving as an *actional* person. The goal of his behavior will be The Other (in the guise of the white man), for The Other alone can give him worth. That is on the ethical level: self-esteem. But there is something else.

I have said that the Negro is phobogenic. What is phobia? I prefer to answer that question by relying on the latest work of Hesnard: "Phobia is a neurosis characterized by the anxious fear of an object (in the broadest sense of anything outside the individual) or, by extension, of a situation."[17] Naturally that object must have certain aspects. It must arouse, Hesnard says, both fear and revulsion. But here we encounter a difficulty. Applying the genetic method to the understanding of phobia, Charles Odier wrote that all anxiety derives from a certain subjective insecurity linked to the absence of the mother.[18]

17. *L'univers morbide de la faute*, p. 37.

18. *Anxiety and Magic Thinking* (New York, International Universities Press, 1956), p. 46. Originally, *L'angoisse et la pensée magique* (Neuchâtel, Delachaux, 1947).

This occurs, according to Odier, sometime in the second year of life.

Investigating the psychic structure of the phobic, he comes to this conclusion: "Before attacking the adult beliefs, all the elements of the infantile structure which produced them must be analyzed."[19] The choice of the phobic object is therefore *overdetermined.* This object does not come at random out of the void of nothingness; in some situation it has previously evoked an affect in the patient. His phobia is the latent presence of this affect at the root of his world; there is an organization that has been given a form. For the object, naturally, need not be there, it is enough that somewhere it *exist*: It is a possibility. This object is endowed with evil intentions and with all the attributes of a malefic power.[20] In the phobic, affect has a priority that defies all rational thinking. As we can see, the phobic is a person who is governed by the laws of rational prelogic and affective prelogic: methods of thinking and feeling that go back to the age at which he experienced the event that impaired his security. The difficulty indicated here is this: Was there a trauma harmful to security in the case of the young woman whom we mentioned a little earlier? In the majority of Negrophobic men has there been an attempt at rape? An attempt at *fellatio?* Proceeding with complete orthodoxy, we should be led by the application of analytic conclusions to this: If an extremely frightening object, such as a more or less imaginary attacker, arouses terror, this is also—for most often such cases are those of women —and especially a terror mixed with sexual revulsion. "I'm afraid of men" really means, at the bottom of the moti-

19. *Ibid.*, p. 76.
20. *Ibid.*, pp. 58 and 68.

vation of the fear, because they might do all kinds of things to me, but not commonplace cruelties: sexual abuses—in other words, immoral and shameful things.[21]

"*Contact* alone is enough to evoke anxiety. For contact is at the same time the basic schematic type of initiating sexual action (touching, caresses—sexuality)."[22] Since we have learned to know all the tricks the ego uses in order to defend itself, we know too that its denials must in no case be taken literally. Are we not now observing a complete inversion? Basically, does this *fear* of rape not itself cry out for rape? Just as there are faces that ask to be slapped, can one not speak of women who ask to be raped? In *If He Hollers Let Him Go,* Chester Himes describes this type very well. The big blonde trembles whenever the Negro goes near her. Yet she has nothing to fear, since the factory is full of white men. In the end, she and the Negro go to bed together.

When I was in military service I had the opportunity to observe the behavior of white women from three or four European countries when they were among Negroes at dances. Most of the time the women made involuntary gestures of flight, of withdrawing, their faces filled with a fear that was not feigned. And yet the Negroes who asked them to dance would have been utterly unable to commit any act at all against them, even if they had wished to do so. The behavior of these women is clearly understandable from the standpoint of imagination. That is because the Negrophobic woman is in fact nothing but a putative sexual partner—just as the Negrophobic man is a repressed homosexual.

---

21. Hesnard, *op. cit.*, p. 38.
22. *Ibid.*, p. 40.

In relation to the Negro, everything takes place on the genital level. A few years ago, I remarked to some friends during a discussion that in a general sense the white man behaves toward the Negro as an elder brother reacts to the birth of a younger. I have since learned that Richard Sterba arrived at the same conclusion in America.

On the phenomenological level there would be a double reality to be observed. The Jew is feared because of his potential for acquisitiveness. "They" are everywhere. The banks, the stock exchanges, the government are infested with "them." "They" control everything. Soon the whole country will belong to "them." "They" do better in examinations than the "real" Frenchmen. Soon "they" will be making the laws for us. Not long ago, an acquaintance studying for the civil service said to me, "Say what you want, 'they' take good care of one another. When Moch was in power, for instance, the number of kikes in government jobs was appalling." In the medical profession the situation is no different. Every Jewish student who wins a prize in a competition does it through "pull." As for the Negroes, they have tremendous sexual powers. What do you expect, with all the freedom they have in their jungles! They copulate at all times and in all places. They are really genital. They have so many children that they cannot even count them. Be careful, or they will flood us with little mulattoes.

Things are indeed going to hell. . . .

The government and the civil service are at the mercy of the Jews.

Our women are at the mercy of the Negroes.

For the sexual potency of the Negro is hallucinating. That is indeed the word: This potency *must be* hallucinating. Psychoanalysts who study the problem soon enough find the mechanisms of every neurosis. Sexual anxiety is predominant here. All the Negrophobic women I have known had abnormal sex lives. Their husbands had left them; or they were widows and they were afraid to find a substitute for the dead husband; or they were divorced and they had doubts at the thought of a new object investment. All of them endowed the Negro with powers that other men (husbands, transient lovers) did not have. And besides there was also an element of perversion, the persistence of infantile formations: God knows how they make love! It must be terrifying.[23]

There is one expression that through time has become singularly eroticized: the black athlete. There is something in the mere idea, one young woman confided to me, that makes the heart skip a beat. A prostitute told me that in her early days the mere thought of going to bed with a Negro brought on an orgasm. She went in search of Negroes and never asked them for money. But, she added, "going to bed with them was no more remarkable

23. In the work of Joachim Marcus we encounter the view according to which the social neurosis—or, if one prefers, abnormal behavior in contact with The Other, whoever he may be—is closely related to the individual situation:

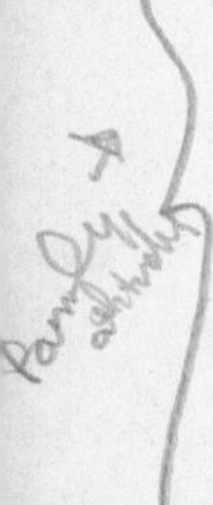

> The study of our questionnaires showed that the most strongly anti-Semitic persons belonged to the most conflictual family structures. Their anti-Semitism was a reaction to frustrations suffered inside the family environment. What demonstrates that the Jew is a substitutive object in anti-Semitism is the fact that, depending on local conditions, the same family situations will produce hatred of Negroes, anti-Catholicism, or anti-Semitism. One can therefore state that, contrary to what is generally believed, it is the attitude that seeks the content rather than the content that creates the attitude. ("Structure familiale et comportements politiques," *op. cit.*, p. 282.)

than going to bed with white men. It was before I did it that I had the orgasm. I used to think about (imagine) all the things they might do to me: and that was what was so terrific."

Still on the genital level, when a white man hates black men, is he not yielding to a feeling of impotence or of sexual inferiority? Since his ideal is an infinite virility, is there not a phenomenon of diminution in relation to the Negro, who is viewed as a penis symbol? Is the lynching of the Negro not a sexual revenge? We know how much of sexuality there is in all cruelties, tortures, beatings. One has only to reread a few pages of the Marquis de Sade to be easily convinced of the fact. Is the Negro's superiority real? Everyone *knows* that it is not. But that is not what matters. The prelogical thought of the phobic has decided that such is the case.[24] Another woman developed a Negrophobia after she had read *J'irai cracher sur vos tombes.* I tried to demonstrate the irrationality of her position by pointing out to her that victimized white women were as sick as the Negro. Besides, I added, this was no case of black vengeance, as the title of the book might seem to imply, because the author was a white man, Boris Vian. I had to accept the futility of all such efforts. That young woman did not want to listen. Anyone who has read the book will understand at once the ambivalence her phobia revealed. I knew a Negro medical student who would not dare to make a vaginal examination of any patient in the gynecological clinic. He told me that one day he had heard one of them

24. To continue in Odier's terminology, it would be more accurate to say "paralogical": "The term 'paralogical' might be suggested for the regression of the neurotic adult." (*Anxiety and Magic Thinking*, p. 118.)

say, "There's a nigger in there. If he touches me, I'll slap his face. You never know with them. He must have great big hands; and besides he's sure to be rough."

If one wants to understand the racial situation psychoanalytically, not from a universal viewpoint but as it is experienced by individual consciousnesses, considerable importance must be given to sexual phenomena. In the case of the Jew, one thinks of money and its cognates. In that of the Negro, one thinks of sex. Anti-Semitism can be rationalized on a basic level. It is because he takes over the country that the Jew is a danger. An acquaintance told me recently that although he was not an anti-Semite he had been constrained to admit that the majority of Jews whom he had known during the war had behaved very badly. I tried in vain to get him to concede that such a statement was the fruit of a determined desire to find the essence of the Jew wherever it might exist.

On a clinical level, I am reminded of the story of the young woman who suffered from a kind of tactile delirium, constantly washing her hands and arms ever since the day a Jew had been introduced to her.

Jean-Paul Sartre has made a masterful study of the problem of anti-Semitism; let us try to determine what are the constituents of Negrophobia. This phobia is to be found on an instinctual, biological level. At the extreme, I should say that the Negro, because of his body, impedes the closing of the postural schema of the white man—at the point, naturally, at which the black man makes his entry into the phenomenal world of the white man. This is not the place in which to state the conclusions I drew from studying the influence exerted on the body by the appearance of another body. (Let us assume, for example, that four fifteen-year-old boys, all more or less athletic, are doing the high jump. One of them wins by jumping four feet ten inches. Then a fifth boy arrives and tops the mark by a half-inch. The four other bodies experience a destructuration.) What is important to us here is to show that with the Negro the cycle of the *biological* begins.[25]

---

25. It would indeed be interesting, on the basis of Lacan's theory of the *mirror period*, to investigate the extent to which the *imago* of his fellow built up in the young white at the usual age would undergo an imaginary aggression with the appearance of the Negro. When one has grasped the mechanism described by Lacan, one can have no further doubt that the real Other for the white man is and will continue to be the black man. And conversely. Only for the white man The Other is perceived on the level of the body image, absolutely as the not-self—that is, the unidentifiable, the unassimilable. For the black man, as we have shown, historical and economic realities come into the picture. "The subject's recognition of his image in the mirror," Lacan says, "is a phenomenon that is doubly significant for the analysis of this stage: The phenomenon appears after six months, and the study of it at that time shows in convincing fashion the tendencies that currently constitute reality for the subject; the mirror image, precisely because of these affinities, affords a good symbol of that reality: of its affective value, illusory like the image, and of its structure, as it reflects the human form." (*Encyclopédie française*, 8-40, 9 and 10.)

We shall see that this discovery is basic: Every time the subject sees his image and recognizes it, it is always in some way "the mental oneness which is inherent in him" that he acclaims. In mental pathology, for instance, when one examines delirious hallucinations or interpretations, one always finds that this self-image is respected. In other words, there is a certain structural harmony, a sum of the individual and of the constructions through which he goes, at every stage of the psychotic behavior. Aside from the fact that this fidelity might be attributed to affective content, there still remains evidence that it would be unscientific to misconstrue. Whenever there is a psychotic belief, there is a reproduction of self. It is especially in the period of anxiety and suspicion described by Dide and Guiraud that The Other takes a hand. At such times it is not surprising to find the Negro in the guise of satyr or mur-

No anti-Semite, for example, would ever conceive of the idea of castrating the Jew. He is killed or sterilized. But the Negro is castrated. The penis, the symbol of manhood, is annihilated, which is to say that it is denied. The difference between the two attitudes is apparent. The Jew is attacked in his religious identity, in his history,

---

derer. But in the stage of systematization, when the conviction is being developed, there is no longer room for a stranger. In extreme cases, moreover, I should not hesitate to say that the theme of the Negro in certain deliriums (when it is not central) ranks with other phenomena such as zooscopy.[a] Lhermitte has described the liberation of the body image. This is what is clinically called heautophany or heautoscopy.[b] The abruptness with which this phenomenon occurs, Lhermitte says, is inordinately strange. It occurs even among normal persons (Goethe, Taine, etc.). I contend that for the Antillean the mirror hallucination is always neutral. When Antilleans tell me that they have experienced it, I always ask the same question: "What color were you?" Invariably they reply: "I had no color." What is more, in hypnagogic hallucinations and in what, by derivation trom Duhamel, is called "salavinization,"[c] the same procedure is repeated. It is not I as a Negro who acts, thinks, and is praised to the skies.

In addition, I suggest that those who are interested in such questions read some of the compositions written in French by Antillean children between the ages of ten and fourteen. Given as a theme "My Feelings Before I Went on Vacation," they reacted like real little Parisians and produced such things as, "I like vacation because then I can run through the fields, breathe fresh air, and come home with *rosy* cheeks." It is apparent that one would hardly be mistaken in saying that the Antillean does not altogether apprehend the fact of his being a Negro. I was perhaps thirteen when for the first time I saw Senegalese soldiers. All I knew about them was what I had heard from veterans of the First World War: "They attack with the bayonet, and, when that doesn't work, they just punch their way through the machine-gun fire with their fists. . . . They cut off heads and collect human ears." These Senegalese were in transit in Martinique, on their way from Guiana. I scoured

in his race, in his relations with his ancestors and with his posterity; when one sterilizes a Jew, one cuts off the source; every time that a Jew is persecuted, it is the whole race that is persecuted in his person. But it is in his corporeality that the Negro is attacked. It is as a concrete personality that he is lynched. It is as an actual being that he is a threat. The Jewish menace is replaced

---

the streets eagerly for a sight of their uniforms, which had been described to me: red scarfs and belts. My father went to the trouble of collecting two of them, whom he brought home and who had the family in raptures. It was the same thing in school. My mathematics teacher, a lieutenant in the reserve who had been in command of a unit of Senegalese troopers in 1914, used to make us shiver with his anecdotes: "When they are praying they must never be disturbed, because then the officers just cease to exist. They're lions in a battle, but you have to respect their habits." There is no reason now to be surprised that Mayotte Capécia dreamed of herself as pink and white: I should say that that was quite normal.

It may perhaps be objected that if the white man is subject to the elaboration of the *imago* of his peer, an analogous phenomenon should occur in the Antillean, visual perception being the sketch for such an elaboration. But to say this is to forget that in the Antilles perception always occurs on the level of the imaginary. It is in white terms that one perceives one's fellows. People will say of someone, for instance, that he is "very black"; there is nothing surprising, within a family, in hearing a mother remark that "X is the blackest of my children"—it means that X is the least white. I can only repeat the observation of a European acquaintance to whom I had explained this: in terms of people, it is nothing but a mystification. Let me point out once more that every Antillean expects all the others to perceive him in terms of the essence of the white man. In the Antilles, just as in France, one comes up against the same myth; a Parisian says, "He is black but he is very intelligent"; a Martinican expresses himself no differently. During the Second World War, teachers went from Guadeloupe to Fort-de-France to correct the examinations of candi-

by the fear of the sexual potency of the Negro. O. Mannoni said:

> An argument widely used by racialists against those who do not share their convictions is worthy of mention for its revealing character. "What," they say, "if you had a daughter, do you mean to say that you would marry her to a negro?" I have seen people who appeared to have no racialist bias lose all critical sense when confronted with this kind of question. The reason is that such an argument disturbs certain uneasy feelings in them (more exactly, *incestuous* feelings) and they turn to racialism as a defence reaction.[26]

---

dates for the baccalaureate, and, driven by curiosity, I went to the hotel where they were staying, simply in order to see Monsieur B., a philosophy teacher who was supposed to be remarkably black; as the Martinicans say, not without a certain irony, he was "blue." One family in particular has an excellent reputation: "They're very black, but they're all quite nice." One of them, in fact, is a piano teacher and a former student at the Conservatoire in Paris, another is a teacher of natural science in the girls' academy, etc. The father was given to walking up and down his balcony every evening at sunset; after a certain time of night, it was always said, he became invisible. Of another family, who lived in the country, it was said that on nights when there was a power failure the children had to laugh so that their parents would know that they were there. On Mondays, very carefully got up in their white linen suits, certain Martinican officials, in the local figure of speech, "looked like prunes in a bowl of milk."

a. Hallucinations of animals. (Translator's note.)

b. The vivid psychological awareness and examination of one's own internal organs as if they were outside oneself—an extreme hypochondria. (Translator's note.)

c. See note 52.

26. [Dominique] O. Mannoni, *Prospero and Caliban: The Psychology of Colonization* (New York, Praeger, 1964), p. 111, note 1.

Before we go further, it seems important to make this point: Granted that unconscious tendencies toward incest exist, why should these tendencies emerge more particularly with respect to the Negro? In what way, taken as an absolute, does a black son-in-law differ from a white son-in-law? Is there not a reaction of unconscious tendencies in both cases? Why not, for instance, conclude that the father revolts because in his opinion the Negro will introduce his daughter into a sexual universe for which the father does not have the key, the weapons, or the attributes?

Every intellectual gain requires a loss in sexual potential. The civilized white man retains an irrational longing for unusual eras of sexual license, of orgiastic scenes, of unpunished rapes, of unrepressed incest. In one way these fantasies respond to Freud's life instinct. Projecting his own desires onto the Negro, the white man behaves "as if" the Negro really had them. When it is a question of the Jew, the problem is clear: He is suspect because he wants to own the wealth or take over the positions of power. But the Negro is fixated at the genital; or at any rate he has been fixated there. Two realms: the intellectual and the sexual. An erection on Rodin's *Thinker* is a shocking thought. One cannot decently "have a hard on" everywhere. The Negro symbolizes the biological danger; the Jew, the intellectual danger.

To suffer from a phobia of Negroes is to be afraid of the biological. For the Negro is only biological. The Negroes are animals. They go about naked. And God alone knows. . . . Mannoni said further: "In his urge to identify the anthropoid apes, Caliban, the Negroes, even the Jews with the mythological figures of the satyrs, man reveals that there are sensitive spots in the human soul at a level[27] where thought becomes confused and where sexual excitement is strangely linked with violence and aggressiveness."[28] Mannoni includes the Jew in his scale. I see nothing inappropriate there. But here the Negro is the master. He is the specialist of this matter: Whoever says *rape* says *Negro.*

Over three or four years I questioned some 500 members of the white race—French, German, English, Italian. I took advantage of a certain air of trust, of relaxation; in each instance I waited until my subject no longer hesitated to talk to me quite openly—that is, until he was sure that he would not offend me. Or else, in the midst of associational tests, I inserted the word *Negro* among some twenty others. Almost 60 per cent of the replies took this form:

Negro brought forth biology, penis, strong, athletic, potent, boxer, Joe Louis, Jesse Owens, Senegalese troops, savage, animal, devil, sin.

Senegalese soldier, used as the stimulus, evoked dreadful, bloody, tough, strong.

It is interesting to note that one in fifty reacted to the word *Negro* with *Nazi* or *SS;* when one knows the emotional meaning of the SS image, one recognizes that the difference from the other answers is negligible. Let me add that some Europeans helped me by giving the test to their acquaintances: In such cases the proportion went up notably. From this result one must acknowledge the

27. When we consider the responses given in waking-dream therapy we shall see that these mythological figures, or "archetypes," do reside very deep in the human mind. Whenever the individual plunges down, one finds the Negro, whether concretely or symbolically.

28. Mannoni, *op. cit.*, p. 111.

effect of my being a Negro: Unconsciously there was a certain reticence.

The Negro symbolizes the biological. First of all, he enters puberty at the age of nine and is a father at the age of ten; he is hot-blooded, and his blood is strong; he is tough. As a white man remarked to me not long ago, with a certain bitterness: "You all have strong constitutions." What a beautiful race—look at the Senegalese. . . . Weren't they called *our Black Devils* during the war? . . . But they must be brutal . . . I just can't see them putting those big hands of theirs on my shoulders. I shudder at the mere thought of it. . . . Well aware that in certain cases one must interpret by opposites, I understand this extra-fragile woman: At bottom what she wants most is to have the powerful Negro bruise her frail shoulders. Sartre says that when one speaks the phrase "a young Jewess," there is an imaginary reek of rape and pillage. . . . Conversely, we might say that the expression "a handsome Negro" contains a "possible" allusion to similar phenomena. I have always been struck by the speed with which "handsome young Negro" turns into "young colt" or "stallion." In the film *Mourning Becomes Electra*, a good part of the plot is based on sexual rivalry. Orin rebukes his sister, Vinnie, because she admired the splendid naked natives of the South Seas. He cannot forgive her for it.[29]

---

29. Let us remember, however, that the situation is ambiguous. Orin is also jealous of his sister's fiancé. On a psychoanalytic level, the film may be described thus: Orin, who suffers from the abandonment-neurosis, is fixated on his mother and is incapable of making a real object investment of his libido. Observe, for instance, his behavior toward the girl to whom he is supposedly engaged. Vinnie, who for her part is fixated on their father, proves to Orin that their mother is unfaithful. But let us not make any mistakes. Her action is a bill of indictment (an introjective mechanism). Supplied with the evidence of the adultery, Orin kills his mother's lover. In reac-

Analysis of the real is always difficult. An investigator can choose between two attitudes toward his subject. First, he can be satisfied only to describe, in the manner of those anatomists who are all surprised when, in the midst of a description of the tibia, they are asked how many fibular depressions *they* have. That is because in their researches there is never a question of themselves but of others. In the beginning of my medical studies, after several nauseating sessions in the dissection room, I asked an older hand how I could prevent such reactions. "My friend, pretend you're dissecting a cat, and everything will be all right. . . ." Second, once he has described reality, the investigator can make up his mind to change it. In principle, however, the decision to describe seems naturally to imply a critical approach and therefore a need to go farther toward some solution. Both authorized and anecdotal literature have created too many stories about Negroes to be suppressed. But putting them all together does not help us in our real task, which is to disclose their mechanics. What matters for us is not to collect facts and behavior, but to find their meaning. Here we can refer to Jaspers, when he wrote: "Comprehension in depth of a single instance will often enable us, phenomenologically, to apply this understanding in general to innumerable cases. Often what one has once grasped is soon met again.

---

tion she commits suicide. Orin's libido, which requires investment in the same manner as before, turns toward Vinnie. In effect, through her behavior and even through her physical appearance, Vinnie takes the place of their mother. Consequently—and this is beautifully handled in the film—Orin becomes an Oedipus in love with his sister. Hence it is understandable that Orin storms lamentation and reproach at his sister when she announces her marriage. But in his conflict with her fiancé it is emotion, affectivity, that he battles; with the Negro, the splendid natives, the conflict lies on a genital, biological level.

What is important in phenomenology is less the study of a large number of instances than the intuitive and deep understanding of a few individual cases."[30] The question that arises is this: Can the white man behave healthily toward the black man and can the black man behave healthily toward the white man?

A pseudo-question, some will say. But when we assert that European culture has an *imago* of the Negro which is responsible for all the conflicts that may arise, we do not go beyond reality. In the chapter on language we saw that on the screen the Negro faithfully reproduces that *imago*. Even serious writers have made themselves its spokesmen. So it was that Michel Cournot could write:

> The black man's sword is a sword. When he has thrust it into your wife, she has really felt something. It is a revelation. In the chasm that it has left, your little toy is lost. Pump away until the room is awash with your sweat, you might as well just be singing. This is *good-by*. . . . Four Negroes with their penises exposed would fill a cathedral. They would be unable to leave the building until their erections had subsided; and in such close quarters that would not be a simple matter.
>
> To be comfortable without problems, they always have the open air. But then they are faced with a constant insult: the palm tree, the breadfruit tree, and so many other proud growths that would not slacken for an empire, erect as they are for all eternity, and piercing heights that are not easily reached at any price.[31]

When one reads this passage a dozen times and lets oneself go—that is, when one abandons oneself to the

30. Karl Jaspers, *Psychopathologie générale*, French translation by Kastler and Mendousse, p. 49.

31. *Martinique* (Paris, Collection Metamorphoses, Gallimard, 1948), pp. 13-14.

movement of its images—one is no longer aware of the Negro but only of a penis; the Negro is eclipsed. He is turned into a penis. He *is* a penis. It is easy to imagine what such descriptions can stimulate in a young girl in Lyon. Horror? Lust? Not indifference, in any case. Now, what is the truth? The average length of the penis among the black men of Africa, Dr. Palès says, rarely exceeds 120 millimeters (4.6244 inches). Testut, in his *Traité d'anatomie humaine,* offers the same figure for the European. But these are facts that persuade no one. The white man is convinced that the Negro is a beast; if it is not the length of the penis, then it is the sexual potency that impresses him. Face to face with this man who is "different from himself," he needs to defend himself. In other words, to personify The Other. The Other will become the mainstay of his preoccupations and his desires.[32] The

32. Some writers have tried, thus accepting prejudices (in the etymological sense of the word), to show why the white man does not understand the sexual life of the Negro. Thus one can find in De Pédrals this passage, which, while it does nevertheless convey the truth, still leaves aside the deep causes of white "opinion":

> The Negro child feels neither surprise nor shame at the facts of reproduction, because he is told whatever he wants to know. It is quite obvious, without having to fall back on the subtleties of psychoanalysis, that this difference cannot help having an effect on his way of thinking and hence on his way of acting. Since the sexual act is presented to him as the most natural, indeed the most commendable thing in view of the end that it pursues—impregnation—the African will retain this outlook as long as he lives; while the European, as long as he lives, will always unconsciously keep alive a guilt complex that neither reason nor experience will ever succeed in altogether dissipating. In this way the African is inclined to view his sexual life as only a part of his physiological life, just like eating, drinking, and sleeping. . . . A conception of this kind, one would suppose, precludes the distortions into which the European is led in order to recon-

prostitute whom I mentioned earlier told me that her hunt for Negroes dated from the time when she had been told this story: One night a woman who was in bed with a Negro went mad; she remained insane for two years, but then when she had been cured refused to go to bed with anyone else. The prostitute did not know what had driven the other woman mad. But she sought furiously to reproduce the same situation, to discover this secret which was part of the ineffable. One must recognize that what she wanted was the destruction, the disolution, of her being on a sexual level. Every experiment that she made with a Negro reinforced her limitations. This delirium of orgasm was unattainable. She could not experience it, so she avenged herself by losing herself in speculation.

One thing must be mentioned in this connection: A white woman who has had a Negro lover finds it difficult to return to white men. Or so at least it is believed, particularly by white men: "Who knows what 'they' can give a woman?" Who indeed does know? Certainly "they" do not. On this subject I cannot overlook this comment by Etiemble:

> Racial jealousy produces the crimes of racism: To many white men, the black is simply that marvelous sword which, once it has transfixed their wives, leaves them forever transfigured. My statistical sources have been able to provide

cile the conflicts of a tortured conscience, a vacillating intellect, and a frustrated instinct. Hence the fundamental difference is not at all of natures, or of constitutions, but of conceptions; hence too the fact that the reproductive instinct, stripped of the halo with which the monuments of our literature have adorned it, is not at all the dominant element in the life of the African as it is in our own, in spite of the statements of *too many students inclined to explain what they have seen by the sole method of analyzing themselves.* (Denis Pierre de Pédrals, *La vie sexuelle en Afrique noire,* Paris, Payot, 1950, pp. 28-29.) My italics—F.F.

> me with no documentation on this point. I have, however, known some Negroes; some white women who have had Negroes; and, finally, some Negro women who have had white lovers. I have heard enough confidences from all of them to be able to deplore the fact that M. Cournot applies his talents to the rejuvenation of a fable in which the white man will always be able to find a specious argument: shameful, dubious, and thus doubly effective.[33]

An endless task, the cataloguing of reality. We accumulate facts, we discuss them, but with every line that is written, with every statement that is made, one has the feeling of incompleteness. Attacking J.-P. Sartre, Gabriel d'Arbousier wrote:

> This anthology, which puts Antilleans, Guianans, Senegalese, and Malagasies on the same footing, creates a deplorable confusion. In this way it states the cultural problem of the overseas countries by detaching it from the historical and social reality of each of them, from the national characteristics and the varying conditions imposed on each of them by imperialist exploitation and oppression. Thus, when Sartre wrote, "Simply by plunging into the depths of his memory as a former slave, the black man asserts that suffering is the lot of man and that it is no less undeserved on that account," did he take into consideration what that might mean for a Hova, a Moor, a Touareg, a Peul, or a Bantu of the Congo or the Ivory Coast?[34]

The objection is valid. It applies to me as well. In the beginning I wanted to confine myself to the Antilles. But, regardless of consequences, dialectic took the upper hand and I was compelled to *see* that the Antillean is first of

---

33. "Sur le *Martinique* de M. Michel Cournot," *Les Temps Modernes*, February, 1950, p. 1505.

34. "Une dangereuse mystification: la théorie de la négritude," *La Nouvelle Revue Critique*, June, 1949.

all a Negro. Nevertheless, it would be impossible to overlook the fact that there are Negroes whose nationality is Belgian, French, English; there are also Negro republics. How can one claim to have got hold of an essential when such facts as these demand one's recognition? The truth is that the Negro race has been scattered, that it can no longer claim unity. When Il Duce's troops invaded Ethiopia, a movement of solidarity arose among men of color. But, though one or two airplanes were sent from America to the invaded country, not a single black man made any practical move. The Negro has a country, he takes his place in a Union or a Commonwealth. Every description should be put on the level of the discrete phenomenon, but here again we are driven out to infinite perspectives. In the universal situation of the Negro there is an ambiguity, which is, however, resolved in his concrete existence. This in a way places him beside the Jew. Against all the arguments I have just cited, I come back to one fact: *Wherever he goes, the Negro remains a Negro.*

In some countries the Negro has entered into the culture. As we have already indicated, it would be impossible to ascribe too much importance to the way in which white children establish contact with the reality of the Negro. In the United States, for example, even if he does not live in the South, where he naturally encounters Negroes concretely, the white child is introduced to them through the myth of Uncle Remus. (In France there is the parallel of *La Case de l'Oncle Tom—Uncle Tom's Cabin.*) Miss Sally's and Marse John's little boy listens with a mixture of fear and admiration to the tales of Br'er Rabbit. To Bernard Wolfe this ambivalence in the white man is the dominant factor in the white American psychology. Relying on the life of Joel Chandler Harris, Wolfe goes so far as to show that the admiration corresponds to a certain identification of the white man with the black. It is perfectly obvious what these stories are all about. Br'er Rabbit gets into conflicts with almost all the other animals in creation, and naturally he is always the winner. These stories belong to the oral tradition of the plantation Negroes. Therefore it is relatively easy to recognize the Negro in his remarkably ironic and wary disguise as a rabbit. In order to protect themselves against their own unconscious masochism, which impels them to rapturous admiration of the (black) rabbit's prowess, the whites have tried to drain these stories of their aggressive potential. This is how they have been able to tell themselves that "the black man makes all the animals behave *like a lower order of human intelligence, the kind that the Negro himself can understand.* The black man naturally feels that *he is in closer touch with the 'lower animals' than with the white man, who is so far superior to him in every respect.*" Others have advanced the theory, with straight faces, that these stories are not reactions to the conditions imposed on the Negro in the United States but are simply *survivals of Africa.* Wolfe gives us the clue to such interpretations:

> On the basis of all the evidence, Br'er Rabbit is an animal because the Negro must be an animal; the rabbit is an outlander because the Negro must be branded as an outlander down to his chromosomes. Ever since slavery began, his Christian and democratic guilt as a slave-owner has led the southerner to describe the Negro as an animal, an unchangeable African whose nature was determined as protoplasm by his "African" genes. If the black man found himself relegated to the Limbo of mankind, he was the victim not of Americans but of the organic inferiority of his jungle ancestors.

So the southerner refused to see in these stories the

aggression that the Negro infused into them. But, Wolfe says, their compiler, Harris, was a psychopath:

> He was especially adept at this task because he was filled to the bursting point with pathological racial obsessions over and above those that tormented the South and, to a lesser degree, all of white America. . . . Indeed, for Harris as well as for many other white Americans, the Negro seemed to be in every respect the opposite of his own anxious self: unworried, gregarious, voluble, muscularly relaxed, never a victim of boredom, or passive, unashamedly exhibitionistic, devoid of self-pity in his condition of concentrated suffering, exuberant. . . .

But Harris always had the feeling of being handicapped. Therefore Wolfe sees him as frustrated—but not after the classic schema: It was the very essence of the man that made it impossible for him to exist in the "natural" way of the Negro. No one had barred him from it; it was just impossible for him. Not prohibited, but unrealizable. And it is because the white man feels himself frustrated by the Negro that he seeks in turn to frustrate the black, binding him with prohibitions of all kinds. And here again the white man is the victim of his unconscious. Let us listen again to Wolfe:

> The Remus stories are a monument to the ambivalence of the South. Harris, the archetype of the southerner, went in search of the Negro's love and claimed that he had won it (the grin of Uncle Remus).[35] But at the same time he was striving for the Negro's hatred (Br'er Rabbit), and he reveled in it, in an unconscious orgy of masochism—very possibly punishing himself for not being the black man, the stereotype of the black man, the prodigious "giver." Is it

35. The character of Uncle Remus was created by Harris. The figure of this gentle, melancholy old slave with his eternal *grin* is one of the most typical images of the American Negro.

not possible that the white South, and perhaps the majority of white America, often behave in the same way in their relations with the Negro?

There is a quest for the Negro, the Negro is in demand, one cannot get along without him, he is needed, but only if he is made palatable in a certain way. Unfortunately, the Negro knocks down the system and breaks the treaties. Will the white man rise in resistance? No, he will adjust to the situation. This fact, Wolfe says, explains why many books dealing with racial problems become best-sellers.[36]

> Certainly no one is *compelled* to read stories of Negroes who make love to white women (*Deep are the Roots, Strange Fruit, Uncle Remus*), of whites who learn that they are Negroes (*Kingsblood Royal, Lost Boundaries, Uncle Remus*), of white men strangled by black men (*Native Son, If He Hollers Let Him Go, Uncle Remus*). . . . We can package the Negro's grin and market it on a grand scale in our popular culture as a cloak for this masochism: The caress sweetens the blow. And, as *Uncle Remus* shows, here the interplay of the races is in large part unconscious. The white man is no more aware of his masochism when he is being titillated by the subtle content of the stereotyped grin than the Negro is aware of his sadism when he transforms the stereotype into a cultural bludgeon. Perhaps less.[37]

In the United States, as we can see, the Negro makes stories in which it becomes possible for him to work off his aggression; the white man's unconscious justifies this aggression and gives it worth by turning it on himself, thus reproducing the classic schema of masochism.[38]

---

36. See also the many Negro films of recent years. And yet all the producers were white.

37. Bernard Wolfe, "L'oncle Rémus et son lapin," *Les Temps Modernes,* May, 1949, pp. 898 ff.

38. It is usual to be told in the United States, when one calls for

We can now stake out a marker. For the majority of white men the Negro represents the sexual instinct (in its raw state). The Negro is the incarnation of a genital potency beyond all moralities and prohibitions. The women among the whites, by a genuine process of induction, invariably view the Negro as the keeper of the impalpable gate that opens into the realm of orgies, of bacchanals, of delirious sexual sensations. . . . We have shown that reality destroys all these beliefs. But they all rest on the level of the imagined, in any case on that of a paralogism. The white man who ascribes a malefic influence to the black is regressing on the intellectual level, since, as we have shown, his perception is based on a mental age of eight years (the comic books). Is there not a concurrent regression to and fixation at pregenital levels of sexual development? Self-castration? (The Negro is taken as a terrifying penis.) Passivity justifying itself by the recognition of the superiority of the black man in terms of sexual capacity? It is obvious what a variety of questions it would be interesting to raise. There are, for instance, men who go to "houses" in order to be beaten by Negroes; passive homosexuals who insist on black partners.

Another solution might be this: There is first of all a sadistic aggression toward the black man, followed by a guilt complex because of the sanction against such behavior by the democratic culture of the country in ques-

---

the real freedom of the Negro: "That's all they're waiting for, to jump our women." Since the white man behaves in an offensive manner toward the Negro, he recognizes that in the Negro's place he would have no mercy on his oppressors. Therefore it is not surprising to see that he identifies himself with the Negro: white "hot-jazz" orchestras, white blues and spiritual singers, white authors writing novels in which the Negro proclaims his grievances, whites in blackface.

tion. This aggression is then tolerated by the Negro: whence masochism. But, I shall be told, your schema is invalid: It does not contain the elements of classic masochism. Perhaps, indeed, this situation is not classic. In any event, it is the only way in which to explain the masochistic behavior of the white man.

From a heuristic point of view, without attributing any reality to it, I should like to propose an explanation of the fantasy: *A Negro is raping me.* From the work of Helene Deutsch[39] and Marie Bonaparte,[40] both of whom took up and in a way carried to their ultimate conclusions Freud's ideas on female sexuality, we have learned that, alternatively clitoral and clitoral-vaginal and finally purely vaginal, a woman—having retained, more or less commingled, her libido in a passive conception and her aggression, having surmounted her double Oedipus complex—proceeds through her biological and psychological growth and arrives at the assumption of her role, which is achieved by neuropsychic integration. We cannot, however, ignore certain failures or certain fixations.

Corresponding to the clitoral stage there is an active Oedipus complex, although, according to Marie Bonaparte, it is not a sequence but a coexistence of the active and the passive. The desexualization of aggression in a girl is less complete than in a boy.[41] The clitoris is perceived as a diminished penis, but, going beyond the concrete, the girl clings only to the quality. She apprehends reality in qualitative terms. In her as in the little boy

39. *The Psychology of Women* (New York, Grune and Stratton, 1944-1945).

40. *Female Sexuality* (New York, International Universities Press, 1953).

41. Marie Bonaparte, "De la sexualité de la femme," in *Revue Française de Psychanalyse*, April-June, 1949.

there will be impulses directed at the mother; she too would like to disembowel the mother.

Our question, then, is whether, side by side with the final achievement of femininity, there is not some survival of this infantile fantasy. "Too strong an aversion in a woman against the rough games of men is, furthermore, a suspicious indication of male protest and excessive bisexuality. It is possible that such a woman will be clitoral."[42] Here is my own view of the matter. First the little girl sees a sibling rival beaten by the father, a libidinal aggressive. At this stage (between the ages of five and nine), the father, who is now the pole of her libido, refuses in a way to take up the aggression that the little girl's unconscious demands of him. At this point, lacking support, this free-floating aggression requires an investment. Since the girl is at the age in which the child begins to enter the folklore and the culture along roads that we know, the Negro becomes the predestined depositary of this aggression. If we go farther into the labyrinth, we discover that when a woman lives the fantasy of rape by a Negro, it is in some way the fulfillment of a private dream, of an inner wish. Accomplishing the phenomenon of turning against self, it is the woman who rapes herself. We can find clear proof of this in the fact that it is commonplace for women, during the sexual act, to cry to their partners: "Hurt me!" They are merely expressing this idea: Hurt me as I would hurt me if I were in your place. The fantasy of rape by a Negro is a variation of this emotion: "I wish the Negro would rip me open as I would have ripped a woman open." Those who grant our conclusions on the psychosexuality of the white woman may ask what we have to say about the woman of color.

42. *Ibid.*, p. 180.

I know nothing about her. What I can offer, at the very least, is that for many women in the Antilles—the type that I shall call the all-but-whites—the aggressor is symbolized by the Senegalese type, or in any event by an inferior (who is so considered).

The Negro is the genital. Is this the whole story? Unfortunately not. The Negro is something else. Here again we find the Jew. He and I may be separated by the sexual question, but we have one point in common. Both of us stand for Evil. The black man more so, for the good reason that he is black. Is not whiteness in symbols always ascribed in French to Justice, Truth, Virginity? I knew an Antillean who said of another Antillean, "His body is black, his language is black, his soul must be black too." This logic is put into daily practice by the white man. The black man is the symbol of Evil and Ugliness.

Henri Baruk, in a recent work on psychiatry,[43] described what he termed the anti-Semitic psychoses.

> In one of my patients the vulgarity and the obscenity of his ravings transcended all that the French language could furnish and took the form of obvious pederastic[44] allusions

---

43. *Précis de psychiatrie* (Paris, Masson, 1950), p. 371.

44. Let me observe at once that I had no opportunity to establish the overt presence of homosexuality in Martinique. This must be viewed as the result of the absence of the Oedipus complex in the Antilles. The schema of homosexuality is well enough known. We should not overlook, however, the existence of what are called there "men dressed like women" or "godmothers." Generally they wear shirts and skirts. But I am convinced that they lead normal sex lives. They can take a punch like any "he-man" and they are not impervious to the allures of women—fish and vegetable merchants. In Europe, on the other hand, I have known several Martinicans who became homosexuals, always passive. But this was by no means a neurotic homosexuality: For them it was a means to a livelihood, as pimping is for others.

with which the patient deflected his inner hatred in transferring it to the scapegoat of the Jews, calling for them to be slaughtered. Another patient, suffering from a fit of delirium aggravated by the events of 1940, had such violent anti-Semitic feelings that one day in a hotel, suspecting the man in the next room to be a Jew, he broke into his room during the night to murder him. . . .

A third patient, with a physically weak constitution—he suffered from chronic colitis—was humiliated by his poor health and ultimately ascribed it to poisoning by means of a "bacterial injection" given to him by one of the male nurses in an institution where he had been earlier—nurses who were anticlerical and Communists, he said, and who had wanted to punish him for his Catholic convictions and utterances. Now that he was in our hospital and safe from "a crew of union men," he felt that he was between Scylla and Charybdis, since he was in the hands of a Jew. By definition this Jew could be only a thief, a monster, a man capable of any and all crimes.

Confronted by such a tide of aggression, this Jew will have to take a stand. Here is all the ambiguity that Sartre describes. Certain pages of *Anti-Semite and Jew* are the finest that I have ever read. The finest, because the problem discussed in them grips us in our guts.[45]

---

45. I am thinking particularly of this passage:

Such then is this haunted man, condemned to make his choice of himself on the basis of false problems and in a false situation, deprived of the metaphysical sense by the hostility of the society that surrounds him, driven to a rationalism of despair. His life is nothing but a long flight from others and from himself. He has been alienated even from his own body; his emotional life has been cut in two; he has been reduced to pursuing the impossible dream of universal brotherhood in a world that rejects him.

Whose is the fault? It is our eyes that reflect to him the unacceptable image that he wishes to dissimulate. It is our words and our gestures—*all* our words and *all* our gestures—our anti-

The Jew, authentic or inauthentic, is struck down by the fist of the "*salaud.*" His situation is such that everything he does is bound to turn against him. For naturally the Jew prefers himself, and it happens that he forgets his Jewishness, or hides it, hides himself from it. That is because he has then admitted the validity of the Aryan system. There are Good and Evil. Evil is Jewish. Everything Jewish is ugly. Let us no longer be Jews. I am no longer a Jew. Down with the Jews. In such circumstances, these are the most aggressive. Like that patient of Baruk who had a persecution complex and who, seeing the doctor one day wearing his yellow star, grabbed him by the lapel and shouted: "I, sir, am a Frenchman." Or this woman: "Making rounds in the ward of my colleague, Dr. Daday, I encountered a Jewish patient who had been the target of taunts and insults from her fellow-patients. A non-Jewish patient had gone to her defense. The Jewish patient thereupon turned on the woman who had defended the Jews, hurling every possible anti-Semitic calumny at her and demanding that that Jewess be got rid of."[46]

This is a fine example of a reactional phenomenon. In order to react against anti-Semitism, the Jew turns him-

---

Semitism, but equally our condescending liberalism—that have poisoned him. It is we who constrain him to choose to be a Jew *whether through flight from himself or through self-assertion;* it is we who force him into the dilemma of Jewish authenticity or inauthenticity. . . . This species that bears witness for essential humanity better than any other because it was born of secondary reactions within the body of humanity—this quintessence of man, disgraced, uprooted, destined from the start to either inauthenticity or martyrdom. In this situation there is not one of us who is not totally guilty and even criminal; the Jewish blood that the Nazis shed falls on all our heads. (Pp. 135-136.)

46. Baruk, *Précis de psychiatrie*, pp. 372-373.

self into an anti-Semite. This is what Sartre presents in *The Reprieve,* in which Birnenschatz finally acts out his disavowal with an intensity that borders on delirium. We shall see that the word is not too strong. Americans who go to Paris are amazed to see so many white women accompanied by Negroes. In New York, Simone de Beauvoir went for a walk with Richard Wright and was rebuked in the street by an old lady. Sartre said: Here it is the Jew, somewhere else it is the Negro. What is essential is a scapegoat. Baruk says nothing different: "Release from hate complexes will be accomplished only if mankind learns to renounce the scapegoat complex."

Fault, Guilt, refusal of guilt, paranoia—one is back in homosexual territory. In sum, what others have described in the case of the Jew applies perfectly in that of the Negro.[47]

Good-Evil, Beauty-Ugliness, White-Black: such are the characteristic pairings of the phenomenon that, making use of an expression of Dide and Guiraud, we shall call "manicheism delirium."[48]

Seeing only one type of Negro, assimilating anti-Semitism to Negrophobia, these seem to be the errors of analysis being committed here. Someone to whom I was talking about this book asked me what I expected to come of it. Ever since Sartre's decisive essay, *What Is Litera-*

---

47. This is what Marie Bonaparte wrote in *Myths de guerre,* No. 1, p. 145: "The anti-Semite projects on to the Jew, ascribes to the Jew all his own more or less unconscious bad instincts. . . . Thus, in ridding himself of them by heaping them on the shoulders of the Jew, he has purged himself of them in his own eyes and sees himself in shining purity. The Jew thus lends himself magnificently to a projection of the Devil. . . . The Negro in the United States assumes the same function of fixation."

48. *Psychiatrie du médecin praticien* (Paris, Masson, 1922), p. 164.

ture?, originally in *Situations II*, literature has been committed more and more to its sole really *contemporary* task, which is to persuade the group to progress to reflection and mediation: This book, it is hoped, will be a mirror with a progressive infrastructure, in which it will be possible to discern the Negro on the road to disalienation.

When there is no longer a "human minimum," there is no culture. It matters very little to me to know that "Muntu means Power" among the Bantu[49]—or at least it might have interested me if certain details had not held me back. What use are reflections on Bantu ontology when one reads elsewhere:

> When 75,000 black miners went on strike in 1946, the state police forced them back to work by firing on them with rifles and charging with fixed bayonets. Twenty-five were killed and thousands were wounded.
>
> At that time Smuts was the head of the government and a delegate to the Peace Conference. On farms owned by white men, the black laborers live almost like serfs. They may have their families with them, but no man is allowed to leave the farm without the permission of his master. If he does so, the police are notified and he is brought back by force and whipped. . . .
>
> Under the Act for Native Administration, the governor-general, as the supreme authority, has autocratic powers over the Africans. By proclamation he may arrest and detain any African deemed dangerous to public order. He may forbid meetings of more than ten persons in any native residential area. The writ of *habeas corpus* is not available to Africans. Mass arrests without warrants are made constantly.
>
> The nonwhite populations of South Africa are at an impasse. All the modern modes of slavery make it impossible

---

49. Reverend Tempels, *La philosophie bantoue.*

> for them to flee from this scourge. In the case of the African especially, white society has smashed his old world without giving him a new one. It has destroyed the traditional tribal foundations of his existence and it blocks the road of the future after having closed the road of the past. . . .
>
> *Apartheid* aspires to banish the Negro from participating in modern history as a free and independent force.[50]

I apologize for this long quotation, but it permits me to bring out some possibilities of black men's mistakes. Alioune Diop, for example, in his introduction to *La philosophie bantoue,* remarks that Bantu ontology knows nothing of the metaphysical misery of Europe. The inference that he draws from this is none the less dangerous:

> The double question that arises is to determine whether the genius of the black man should cultivate what constitutes his individuality, that youth of spirit, that innate respect for man and creation, that joy in living, that peace which is not a disfigurement of man imposed and suffered through moral hygiene, but a natural harmony with the happy majesty of life. . . . One wonders too what the Negro can contribute to the modern world. . . . What we can say is that the very idea of culture conceived as a revolutionary will is as contrary to our genius as the very idea of progress. Progress would have haunted our consciousness only if we had grievances against life, which is a gift of nature.

Be careful! It is not a matter of finding Being in Bantu thought, when Bantu existence subsists on the level of nonbeing, of the imponderable.[51] It is quite true that Bantu philosophy is not going to open itself to understanding through a revolutionary will: But it is precisely in that degree in which Bantu society, being a closed

50. I. R. Skine, "Apartheid en Afrique du Sud," *Les Temps Modernes,* July, 1950.

51. See, for example, *Cry, the Beloved Country,* by Alan Paton.

society, does not contain that substitution of the exploiter for the ontological relations of Forces. Now we know that Bantu society no longer exists. And there is nothing ontological about segregation. Enough of this rubbish.

For some time there has been much talk about the Negro. A little too much. The Negro would like to be dropped, so that he may regroup his forces, his authentic forces.

One day he said: "My negritude is neither a tower. . . ."

And someone came along to Hellenize him, to make an Orpheus of him . . . this Negro who is looking for the universal. He is looking for the universal! But in June, 1950, the hotels of Paris refused to rent rooms to Negro pilgrims. Why? Purely and simply because their Anglo-Saxon customers (who are rich and who, as everyone knows, hate Negroes) threatened to move out.

The Negro is aiming for the universal, but on the screen his Negro essence, his Negro "nature," is kept intact:

> always a servant
> always obsequious and smiling
> me never steal, me never lie
> eternally 'sho' good eatin'. . . .

The Negro is universalizing himself, but at the Lycée Saint-Louis, in Paris, one was thrown out: He had had the impudence to read Engels.

There is a drama there, and the black intellectuals are running the risk of being trapped by it.

What? I have barely opened eyes that had been blindfolded, and someone already wants to drown me in the universal? What about the others? Those who "have no voice," those who "have no spokesman." . . . I need to lose myself in my negritude, to see the fires, the segregations, the repressions, the rapes, the discriminations, the boycotts. We need to put our fingers on every sore that mottles the black uniform.

One can already imagine Alioune Diop wondering what place the black genius will have in the universal chorus. It is my belief that a true culture cannot come to life under present conditions. It will be time enough to talk of the black genius when the man has regained his rightful place.

Once again I come back to Césaire; I wish that many black intellectuals would turn to him for their inspiration. I must repeat to myself too: "And more than anything, my body, as well as my soul, do not allow yourself to cross your arms like a sterile spectator, for life is not a spectacle, for a sea of sorrows is not a stage, for a man who cries out is not a dancing bear. . . ."

Continuing to take stock of reality, endeavoring to ascertain the instant of symbolic crystallization, I very naturally found myself on the threshold of Jungian psychology. European civilization is characterized by the presence, at the heart of what Jung calls the collective unconscious, of an archetype: an expression of the bad instincts, of the darkness inherent in every ego, of the uncivilized savage, the Negro who slumbers in every white man. And Jung claims to have found in uncivilized peoples the same psychic structure that his diagram portrays. Personally, I think that Jung has deceived himself. Moreover, all the peoples that he has known—whether the Pueblo Indians of Arizona or the Negroes of Kenya in British East Africa—have had more or less traumatic contacts with the white man. I said earlier that in his Salavinizations[52]

---

52. Salavin is a character created by Georges Duhamel, and who is the prototype of the ineffectual man: a mediocrity, a creature of fleeting impulse, and always the victim of his own chimeras. (Translator's note.)

the young Antillean is never black; and I have tried to show what this phenomenon corresponds to. Jung locates the collective unconscious in the inherited cerebral matter. But the collective unconscious, without our having to fall back on the genes, is purely and simply the sum of prejudices, myths, collective attitudes of a given group. It is taken for granted, to illustrate, that the Jews who have settled in Israel will produce in less than a hundred years a collective unconscious different from the ones that they had had before 1945 in the countries which they were forced to leave.

On the level of philosophic discussion, this would be the place to bring up the old problem of instinct and habit: instinct, which is inborn (we know how we must view this "innateness"), invariable, specific; habit, which is acquired. On this level one would have only to demonstrate that Jung has confused instinct and habit. In his view, in fact, the collective unconscious is bound up with the cerebral structure, the myths and archetypes are permanent engrams of the race. I hope I have shown tha. nothing of the sort is the case and that in fact the collective unconscious is cultural, which means acquired. Just as a young mountaineer of the Carpathians, under the physico-chemical conditions of his country, is likely to develop a myxedema, so a Negro like René Maran, who has lived in France and breathed and eaten the myths and prejudices of racist Europe, and assimilated the collective unconscious of that Europe, will be able, if he stands outside himself, to express only his hatred of the Negro. One must move softly, and there is a whole drama in having to lay bare little by little the workings of processes that are seen in their totality. Will this statement be susceptible of understanding? *In Europe, the black man is the symbol of Evil.* One must move softly,

I know, but it is not easy. The torturer is the black man, Satan is black, one talks of shadows, when one is dirty one is black—whether one is thinking of physical dirtiness or of moral dirtiness. It would be astonishing, if the trouble were taken to bring them all together, to see the vast number of expressions that make the black man the equivalent of sin. In Europe, whether concretely or symbolically, the black man stands for the bad side of the character. As long as one cannot understand this fact, one is doomed to talk in circles about the "black problem." Blackness, darkness, shadow, shades, night, the labyrinths of the earth, abysmal depths, blacken someone's reputation; and, on the other side, the bright look of innocence, the white dove of peace, magical, heavenly light. A magnificent blond child—how much peace there is in that phrase, how much joy, and above all how much hope! There is no comparison with a magnificent black child: literally, such a thing is unwonted. Just the same, I shall not go back into the stories of black angels. In Europe, that is to say, in every civilized and civilizing country, the Negro is the symbol of sin. The archetype of the lowest values is represented by the Negro. And it is exactly the same antinomy that is encountered in Desoille's *waking dreams*. How else is one to explain, for example, that the unconscious representing the base and inferior traits is colored black? With Desoille, in whose work the situation is (without any intention of a pun) clearer, it is always a matter of descending or climbing. When I descend I see caverns, grottoes where savages dance. Let there be no mistake, above all. For example, in one of the waking-dream sessions that Desoille describes for us, we find Gauls in a cave. But, it must be pointed out, the Gaul is a simple fellow. A Gaul in a cave, it is almost like a family picture—a result, perhaps, of "our ancestors, the

Gauls." I believe it is necessary to become a child again in order to grasp certain psychic realities. This is where Jung was an innovator: He wanted to go back to the childhood of the world, but he made a remarkable mistake: He went back only to the childhood of Europe.

In the remotest depth of the European unconscious an inordinately black hollow has been made in which the most immoral impulses, the most shameful desires lie dormant. And as every man climbs up toward whiteness and light, the European has tried to repudiate this uncivilized self, which has attempted to defend itself. When European civilization came into contact with the black world, with those savage peoples, everyone agreed: Those Negroes were the principle of evil.

Jung consistently identifies the foreign with the obscure, with the tendency to evil: He is perfectly right. This mechanism of projection—or, if one prefers, transference—has been described by classic psychoanalysis. In the degree to which I find in myself something unheard-of, something reprehensible, only one solution remains for me: to get rid of it, to ascribe its origin to someone else. In this way I eliminate a short circuit that threatens to destroy my equilibrium. One must be careful with waking dreams in the early sessions, because it is not good if the obscenity emerges too soon. The patient must come to understand the workings of sublimation before he makes any contact with the unconscious. If a Negro comes up in the first session, he must be removed at once; to that end, suggest a stairway or a rope to the patient, or propose that he let himself be carried off in a helicopter. Infallibly, the Negro will stay in his hole. In Europe the Negro has one function: that of symbolizing the lower emotions, the baser inclinations, the dark side of the soul. In the collective unconscious of *homo occidentalis*, the Negro—or, if one prefers, the color black—symbolizes evil, sin, wretchedness, death, war, famine. All birds of prey are black. In Martinique, whose collective unconscious makes it a European country, when a "blue" Negro—a coal-black one—comes to visit, one reacts at once: "What bad luck is he bringing?"

The collective unconscious is not dependent on cerebral heredity; it is the result of what I shall call the unreflected imposition of a culture. Hence there is no reason to be surprised when an Antillean exposed to waking-dream therapy relives the same fantasies as a European. It is because the Antillean partakes of the same collective unconscious as the European.

If what has been said thus far is grasped, this conclusion may be stated: It is normal for the Antillean to be anti-Negro. Through the collective unconscious the Antillean has taken over all the archetypes belonging to the European. The *anima* of the Antillean Negro is almost always a white woman. In the same way, the *animus* of the Antilleans is always a white man. That is because in the works of Anatole France, Balzac, Bazin, or any of the rest of "our" novelists, there is never a word about an ethereal yet ever present black woman or about a dark Apollo with sparkling eyes. . . . But I too am guilty, here I am talking of Apollo! There is no help for it: I am a white man. For unconsciously I distrust what is black in me, that is, the whole of my being.

I am a Negro—but of course I do not know it, simply because I am one. When I am at home my mother sings me French love songs in which there is never a word about Negroes. When I disobey, when I make too much noise, I am told to "stop acting like a nigger."

Somewhat later I read white books and little by little I take into myself the prejudices, the myths, the folklore that have come to me from Europe. But I will not accept them all, since certain prejudices do not apply in the Antilles. Anti-Semitism, for instance, does not exist there, for there are no Jews, or virtually none. Without turning to the idea of collective catharsis, it would be easy for me to show that, without thinking, the Negro selects himself as an object capable of carrying the burden of original sin. The white man chooses the black man for this function, and the black man who is white also chooses the black man. The black Antillean is the slave of this cultural imposition. After having been the slave of the white man, he enslaves himself. The Negro is in every sense of the word a victim of white civilization. It is not surprising that the artistic creations of Antillean poets bear no special watermark: These men are white. To come back to psychopathology, let us say that the Negro lives an ambiguity that is extraordinarily neurotic. At the age of twenty—at the time, that is, when the collective unconscious has been more or less lost, or is resistant at least to being raised to the conscious level—the Antillean recognizes that he is living an error. Why is that? Quite simply because—and this is very important—the Antillean has recognized himself as a Negro, but, by virtue of an ethical transit, he also feels (collective unconscious) that one is a Negro to the degree to which one is wicked, sloppy, malicious, instinctual. Everything that is the opposite of these Negro modes of behavior is white. This must be recognized as the source of Negrophobia in the Antillean. In the collective unconscious, black = ugliness, sin, darkness, immorality. In other words, he is Negro who is immoral. If I order my life like that of a moral man, I simply am not a Negro. Whence the Martinican custom of saying of a worthless white man that he has "a nigger soul." Color is nothing, I do not even notice it, I know only one thing, which is the purity of my conscience and the whiteness of my soul. "Me white like snow," the other said.

Cultural imposition is easily accomplished in Martinique. The ethical transit encounters no obstacle. But the real white man is waiting for me. As soon as possible he will tell me that it is not enough to try to be white, but that a white totality must be achieved. It is only then that I shall recognize the betrayal. —Let us conclude. An Antillean is made white by the collective unconscious, by a large part of his individual unconscious, and by the virtual totality of his mechanism of individuation. The color of his skin, of which there is no mention in Jung, is black. All the inabilities to understand are born of this blunder.

While he was in France, studying for his degree in literature, Césaire "discovered his cowardice." He knew that it was cowardice, but he could never say why. He felt that it was ridiculous, idiotic, I might say even unhealthy, but in none of his writings can one trace the mechanism of that cowardice. That is because what was necessary was to shatter the current situation and to try to apprehend reality with the soul of a child. The Negro in the streetcar was funny and ugly. Certainly Césaire laughed at him. That was because there was nothing in common between himself and this authentic Negro. A handsome Negro is introduced to a group of white Frenchmen. If it is a group of intellectuals, we can be sure that the Negro will try to assert himself. He will insist that attention be paid not to the color of his skin but to the force of his intellect. There are many people in Martinique who at the age of twenty or thirty begin to steep themselves in Montesquieu or Claudel for the sole purpose of being able to quote them. That is because, through their knowledge of these writers, they expect their color to be forgotten.

Moral consciousness implies a kind of scission, a fracture of consciousness into a bright part and an opposing black part. In order to achieve morality, it is essential that the black, the dark, the Negro vanish from consciousness. Hence a Negro is forever in combat with his own image.

If in like manner one allows M. Hesnard his scientific conception of the moral life, and if the world of moral sickness is to be understood by starting from Fault and Guilt, a normal person will be one who has freed himself of this guilt, or who in any case has managed not to submit to it. More directly, each individual has to charge the blame for his baser drives, his impulses, to the account of an evil genius, which is that of the culture to which he belongs (we have seen that this is the Negro). This collective guilt is borne by what is conventionally called the scapegoat. Now the scapegoat for white society—which is based on myths of progress, civilization, liberalism, education, enlightenment, refinement—will be precisely the force that opposes the expansion and the triumph of these myths. This brutal opposing force is supplied by the Negro.

In the society of the Antilles, where the myths are identical with those of the society of Dijon or Nice, the young Negro, identifying himself with the civilizing power, will make the nigger the scapegoat of his moral life.

I was fourteen years old when I began to understand the meaning of what I now call cultural imposition. I had an acquaintance, now dead, whose father, an Italian, had married a Martinican. This man had lived in Fort-de-France for more than twenty years. He was considered an Antillean, but, underneath, his origin was always remembered. Now, in France, from a military point of view, an Italian is despised; one Frenchmen is the equal of ten

Italians; the Italians have no guts. . . . My acquaintance had been born in Martinique and he associated only with Martinicans. On the day Montgomery routed the Italian army at Bengazi, I wanted to mark the Allies' victory on my map. Measuring the substantial advance of the lines, I could not help exulting: "We really murdered them!" My acquaintance, who was not unaware of his father's origin, was extremely embarrassed. For that matter, so was I. Both of us were victims of a cultural imposition. I am convinced that anyone who has grasped this phenomenon and all its consequences will know exactly in what direction to look for the solution. Listen to the Rebel of Césaire:

"It is rising . . . it is rising from the depths of the earth . . . the black tide is rising . . . waves of cries . . . bogs of animal odors . . . the raging storm of naked feet . . . and the paths of the cliffs are teeming with more, they clamber down the sides of ravines where obscene savage torrents pour impregnation into chaotic rivers, seas of corruption, oceans in convulsion, amid a black laughter of knives and bad alcohol. . . ."

Do you understand? Césaire has *come down.* He is ready to see what is happening at the very depths, and now he can go up. He is ripe for the dawn. But he does not leave the black man down there. He lifts him to his own shoulders and raises him to the clouds. Earlier, in *Cahier d'un retour au pays natal,* he had prepared us. What he has chosen is, to use the expression of Gaston Bachelard,[53] a psyche of ascent:

> and for this, O lord with white teeth, men
> with fragile necks
> receive and collect fatal calm triangular

53. *L'air et les songes* (Paris, Corti, 1943).

and for me my dances
my bad-nigger dances
for me my dances
break-the-yoke dance
jail-break dance
it-is-fine-and-good-and-right-to-be-a-Negro dance
For me my dances and let the sun bounce off the racket
of my hands
no the unjust sun is no longer enough for me
twist yourself, wind, round my new growth
touch my spaced fingers
I give you my conscience and its rhythm of flesh
I give you the flames that char my weakness
I give you the chain-gang
I give you the swamp
I give you the Intourist with the three-cornered journey
devour wind
I give you my rugged lips
devour and twist yourself
and twisting clasp me in a greater shiver
embrace me into the fury of us
embrace, embrace US
but biting us as well
into the blood of our blood bitten
embrace, my purity has no bond but your
purity
but then embrace
like a field of measured *filaos*
the evening
our many-colored purities
and bind, bind me without remorse
bind me with your great arms to the glowing clay
bind my black vibration to the very navel
of the world
bind, bind me bitter brotherhood
then, strangling me with your lasso of stars
rise, Dove

rise
rise
rise
I follow you who are imprinted on my ancestral
white cornea
rise glutton of the sky
and the vast black hole where I wanted to drown myself
the other moon
there now I want to haul out the evil tongue
of the night in its moveless glaze![54]

One can understand why Sartre views the adoption of a Marxist position by black poets as the logical conclusion of Negrohood. In effect, what happens is this: As I begin to recognize that the Negro is the symbol of sin, I catch myself hating the Negro. But then I recognize that I am a Negro. There are two ways out of this conflict. Either I ask others to pay no attention to my skin, or else I want them to be aware of it. I try then to find value for what is bad—since I have unthinkingly conceded that the black man is the color of evil. In order to terminate this neurotic situation, in which I am compelled to choose an unhealthy, conflictual solution, fed on fantasies, hostile, inhuman in short, I have only one solution: to rise above this absurd drama that others have staged round me, to reject the two terms that are equally unacceptable, and, through one human being, to reach out for the universal. When the Negro dives—in other words, goes under—something remarkable occurs.

Listen again to Césaire:

Ho ho
Their power is well anchored
Gained

54. Aimé Césaire, *Cahier d'un retour au pays natal* (Paris, Présence Africaine, 1956), pp. 94-96.

Needed
My hands bathe in bright heather
In swamps of annatto trees
My gourd is heavy with stars
But I am weak. Oh I am weak.
Help me.
And here I am on the edge of metamorphosis
Drowned blinded
Frightened of myself, terrified of myself
Of the gods . . . you are no gods. I am free.

THE REBEL: I have a pact with this night, for twenty years
I have heard it calling softly for me. . . .[55]

Having again discovered that night, which is to say the sense of his identity, Césaire learned first of all that "it is no use painting the foot of the tree white, the strength of the bark cries out from beneath the paint. . . ."

Then, once he had laid bare the white man in himself, he killed him:

> We broke down the doors. The master's room was wide open. The master's room was brilliantly lighted, and the master was there, quite calm . . . and we stopped. . . . He was the master. . . . I entered. "It is you," he said to me, quite calmly. . . . It was I. It was indeed I, I told him, the good slave, the faithful slave, the slavish slave, and suddenly his eyes were two frightened cockroaches on a rainy day . . . I struck, the blood flowed: That is the only *baptism* that I remember today.[56]

"After an unexpected and salutary internal revolution, he now paid tribute to his own revolting ugliness."[57]

55. *Et les chiens se taisaient*, a tragedy, in *Les Armes Miraculeuses* (Paris, Gallimard, 1946), pp. 144 and 122.
56. *Ibid.*, p. 136.
57. *Ibid.*, p. 65.

What more is there to add? After having driven himself to the limit of self-destruction, the Negro is about to leap, whether deliberately or impetuously, into the "black hole" from which will come "the great Negro cry with such force that the pillars of the world will be shaken by it."

The European knows and he does not know. On the level of reflection, a Negro is a Negro; but in the unconscious there is the firmly fixed image of the nigger-savage. I could give not a dozen but a thousand illustrations. Georges Mounin said in *Présence Africaine*: "I had the good luck not to discover the Negroes through Lévy-Bruhl's *Mentalité primitive* read in a sociology course; more broadly, I had the good luck to discover the Negroes otherwise than through books—and I am grateful for it every day. . . ."[58]

Mounin, whom it would be impossible to take for an average Frenchman, added, and thus rose inestimably in my opinion: "I profited perhaps by learning, at an age when one's mind has not yet been prejudiced, that Negroes are men like ourselves. . . . I as a white man thus gained, perhaps, the possibility of always being natural with a Negro—and never, in his presence, to fall stupidly and imperceptibly into that attitude of ethnographic investigator that is still too often our unbearable manner of *putting them in their place*. . . ."

In the same issue of *Présence Africaine*, Émile Dermenghem, who cannot be accused of Negrophobia, said: "One of my childhood memories is of a visit to the World's

58. Premières réponses à l'enquête sur le "Mythe du nègre," *Présence Africaine*, No. 2.

Fair of 1900, during which my chief enthusiasm was to see a Negro. My imagination had naturally been stimulated by my reading: *Capitaine de quinze ans* (A Captain at Fifteen), *Les Aventures de Robert* (Robert's Adventures), *Les Voyages de Livingstone* (Livingstone's Travels)." Dermenghem tells us that this was the manifestation of his taste for the exotic. While I may be prepared to put my two hands into his and believe the Dermenghem who wrote the article, I ask his permission to entertain doubts about the Dermenghem of the 1900 Fair.

I should be annoyed with myself if I were simply picking up old subjects that had been worked dry for fifty years. To write about the chances for Negro friendship is an unselfish undertaking, but unfortunately the Negrophobes and the other princes consort are impregnable to unselfishness. When we read, "The Negro is a savage, and to lead savages there is only one method: a kick in the butt," we sit at our desks and we like to think that "all such idiocies will have to die out." But everyone is in agreement on that. To quote *Présence Africaine* (No. 5) again, Jacques Howlett wrote there:

> Two things, furthermore, it seems, contributed to the aversion toward the Negro in the world of the other, which are impossible for me to comprehend: the color of his skin and his nakedness, for I pictured the Negro naked. Certainly, superficial factors (although one cannot be sure to what extent they continue to haunt our new ideas and our altered conceptions) could sometimes mask that remote black and naked being, almost nonexistent; such as the nice Negro with the red army tarboosh and the infinite Fernandel-like grin, the symbol of some chocolate confection; or the brave Senegalese *pioupiou*, "a slave to his orders," a Don Quixote without glory, "a good-fellow hero" with all that

stems from the "epic of empire"; or the Negro "waiting for salvation," the "submissive child" of a bearded missionary.

Farther on, Jacques Howlett tells us that as a reaction he made the Negro his symbol of innocence. He tells us the reason why, but we have to remember that he was no longer eight years old, for he speaks of "a bad conscience about sexuality" and about "solipsism." I am convinced, however, as far as that "innocence for a grown man" is concerned, that Jacques Howlett has left it far, far behind him.

Beyond all question the most interesting testimony is presented by Michel Salomon. Although he defends himself against the charge, he stinks of racism. He is a Jew, he has a "millennial experience of anti-Semitism," and yet he is a racist. Listen to him: "But to say that the mere fact of his skin, of his hair, of that aura of sensuality that he [the Negro] gives off, does not spontaneously give rise to a certain embarrassment, whether of attraction or of revulsion, is to reject the facts in the name of a ridiculous prudery that has never solved anything. . . ." Later he goes to the extreme of telling us about the "prodigious vitality of the black man."

M. Salomon's study informs us that he is a physician. He should be wary of those literary points of view that are unscientific. The Japanese and the Chinese are ten times more prolific than the Negro: Does that make them sensual? And in addition, M. Salomon, I have a confession to make to you: I have never been able, without revulsion, to hear a *man* say of another man: "He is so sensual!" I do not know what the sensuality of a man is. Imagine a woman saying of another woman: "She's so terribly desirable—she's darling. . . ." The Negro, M.

Salomon, gives off no aura of sensuality either through his skin or through his hair. It is just that over a series of long days and long nights the image of the biological-sexual-sensual-genital-nigger has imposed itself on you and you do not know how to get free of it. The *eye* is not merely a mirror, but a correcting mirror. The *eye* should make it possible for us to correct cultural errors. I do not say the *eyes,* I say the *eye,* and there is no mystery about what that eye refers to; not to the crevice in the skull but to that very uniform light that wells out of the reds of Van Gogh, that glides through a concerto of Tschaikowsky, that fastens itself desperately to Schiller's *Ode to Joy,* that allows itself to be conveyed by the worm-ridden bawling of Césaire.

The Negro problem does not resolve itself into the problem of Negroes living among white men but rather of Negroes exploited, enslaved, despised by a colonialist, capitalist society that is only accidentally white. You wonder, M. Salomon, what you would do "if you had 800,000 Negroes in France"; because for you there is a problem, the problem of the increase of Negroes, the problem of the Black Peril. The Martinican is a Frenchman, he wants to remain part of the French Union, he asks only one thing, he wants the idiots and the exploiters to give him the chance to live like a human being. I can imagine myself lost, submerged in a white flood composed of men like Sartre or Aragon, I should like nothing better. You say, M. Salomon, that there is nothing to be gained by caution, and I share your view. But I do not feel that I should be abandoning my personality by marrying a European, whoever she might be; I can tell you that I am making no "fool's bargains." If my children are suspected, if the crescents of their fingernails are inspected, it will be simply because society will not have changed, because, as you so well put it, society will have kept its mythology intact. For my part, I refuse to consider the problem from the standpoint of *either-or*. . . .

What is all this talk of a black people, of a Negro nationality? I am a Frenchman. I am interested in French culture, French civilization, the French people. We refuse to be considered "outsiders," we have full part in the French drama. When men who were not basically bad, only deluded, invaded France in order to subjugate her, my position as a Frenchman made it plain to me that my place was not outside but in the very heart of the problem. I am personally interested in the future of France, in French values, in the French nation. What have I to do with a black empire?

Georges Mounin, Dermenghem, Howlett, Salomon have all tried to find answers to the question of the origin of the myth of the Negro. All of them have convinced us of one thing. It is that an authentic grasp of the reality of the Negro could be achieved only to the detriment of the cultural crystallization.

Recently, in a children's paper, I read a caption to a picture in which a young black Boy Scout was showing a Negro village to three or four white scouts: "This is the kettle where my ancestors cooked yours." One will gladly concede that there are no more Negro cannibals, but we should not allow ourselves to forget. . . . Quite seriously, however, I think that the writer of that caption has done a genuine service to Negroes without knowing it. For the white child who reads it will not form a mental picture of the Negro in the act of eating the white man, but rather as having eaten him. Unquestionably, this is progress.

Before concluding this chapter, I should like to abstract a case study, for access to which I must thank the medical director of the women's division of the psychiatric hospital of Saint-Ylie. The case clarifies the point of view that I am defending here. It proves that, at its extreme, the myth of the Negro, the idea of the Negro, can become the decisive factor of an authentic alienation.

Mlle. B. was nineteen years old when she entered the hospital in March. Her admission sheet reads:

> The undersigned, Dr. P., formerly on the staff of the Hospitals of Paris, certifies that he has examined Mlle. B., who is afflicted with a nervous disease consisting of periods of agitation, motor instability, tics, and spasms which are conscious but which she cannot control. These symptoms have been increasing and prevent her from leading a normal social life. Her commitment for observation is required under the provisions laid down by the law of 1838 regarding voluntary commitments.

Twenty-four hours later the chief physican found these facts: "Afflicted with neurotic tics that began at the age of ten and became aggravated at the onset of puberty, and further when she began going to work away from home. Intermittent depressions with anxiety, accompanied by a recrudescence of these symptoms. Obesity. Requests treatment. Feels reassured in company. Assigned to an open ward. Should remain institutionalized."

Her immediate family had no history of pathological manifestations. Puberty occurred at the age of sixteen. A physical examination showed nothing except adiposity and a minimal epidermal indication of a slight endocrine insufficiency. Her menstrual periods were regular.

An interview made it possible to isolate these details: "It's especially when I'm working that the tics come."

(The patient was working at a job that entailed her living away from home.) The tics affected the eyes and the forehead; she panted and yelped. She slept quite well, without nightmares, and ate well. She was not out of sorts during menstruation. When she went to bed, the facial tics were constant until she fell asleep.

The observations of the ward nurse: "It is worst when she is alone. When she is talking with others, or is merely with them, it is less noticeable. The tic depends on what she is doing. She begins by tapping both her feet, and then goes on to raise her feet, her legs, her arms, her shoulders symmetrically."

She uttered sounds. It was never possible to understand what she was saying. This manifestation ended in quite loud, inarticulate cries. As soon as she was spoken to, these stopped.

The psychiatrist in charge decided to employ waking-dream therapy. A preliminary interview had brought out the existence of hallucinations in the form of terrifying circles, and the patient had been asked to describe them. Here is an excerpt from the notes on the first session:

> Deep and concentric, the circles expanded and contracted to the rhythm of a Negro tom-tom. This tom-tom made the patient think of the danger of losing her parents, especially her mother.
>
> I then asked her to make the sign of the cross over these circles, but they did not disappear. I told her to take a cloth and rub them out, and they vanished.
>
> She turned in the direction of the tom-tom. She was surrounded by half-naked men and women dancing in a frightening way. I told her not to be afraid to join the dance. She did so. Immediately the appearance of the dancers changed.

It was a splendid party. The men and women were well dressed and they were dancing a waltz, *The Snow Star*.

I told her to go closer to the circles; she could no longer see them. I told her to think of them; they appeared, but they were broken. I told her to go in through the opening. "I'm not completely surrounded any more," she said spontaneously, "I can get out again." The circle broke into two pieces and then into several. Soon there were only two pieces, and then they disappeared. There were frequent throat and eye tics while she was talking.

A succession of such sessions will bring about the sedation of the motor disturbance.

Here are notes on another session:

I told her to bring back the circles. She could not see them at first; then they came. They were broken. She entered them. They broke, rose again, then gently, one after another, fell away into the void. I told her to listen to the tom-tom. She did not hear it. She called to it. She heard it on the left.

I suggested to her that an angel would go with her to the tom-tom: She wanted to go all alone. But someone was coming down from the sky. It was an angel. He was smiling; he took her close to the tom-tom. There were only black men there, and they were dancing round a large fire and looked evil. The angel asked her what they were going to do; she said they were going to burn a white man. She looked for him everywhere. She could not see him.

"Ah, I see him! He's a white man about fifty years old. He's half undressed."

The angel began to negotiate with the black chief (for she was afraid). The black chief said that this white man was not from their country and so they were going to burn him. But he had done nothing wrong.

They set him free and went back to their dancing, joyfully. She refused to take part in the dance.

I sent her to talk to the chief. He was dancing alone. The white man had disappeared. She wanted to go away and seemed to have no desire to know the Negroes. She wanted to go away with her angel, somewhere where she would really be at home, with her mother, her brothers, and her sisters.

When the tics had ceased, the treatment was dropped. A few days later the patient was seen again because she had had a relapse. These are the notes of that session:

The circles kept coming closer. She hit them with a stick. They broke into fragments. The stick was a magic wand. It changed these bits of iron into something shining and beautiful.

She turned toward a fire. It was the fire round which the Negroes were dancing. She wanted to know the chief, and she approached him.

One Negro who had stopped dancing started again, but in a new rhythm. She danced round the fire and let the Negroes take her hands.

These sessions have clearly improved her condition. She writes to her parents, receives visits, goes to the film showings in the hospital. She takes part in group games. Now, when some other patient plays a waltz on the piano in the day room, this patient asks others to dance with her. She is popular and respected among the other patients.

I take this passage from the notes of another session:

She began to think about the circles again. Each was broken into a single piece, on the right of which something was missing. The smaller circles remained intact. She wanted to break them. She took them in her hands and bent them, and then they broke. One, however, was still left. She went through it. On the other side she found she was in darkness. But she was not afraid. She called someone and her guardian angel came down, friendly and smiling. He led her to the right, back into the daylight.

In this case, the waking-dream therapy produced appreciable results. But as soon as the patient was once more *alone* the tics returned.

I do not want to elaborate on the infrastructure of this psychoneurosis. The questions put by the chief psychiatrist had brought out a fear of imaginary Negroes—a fear first experienced at the age of twelve.

I had a great many talks with this patient. When she was ten or twelve years old, her father, "an old-timer in the Colonial Service," liked to listen to programs of Negro music. The tom-tom echoed through their house every evening, long after she had gone to bed. Besides, as we have pointed out, it is at this age that the savage-cannibal-Negro makes his appearance. The connection was easily discernible.

In addition, her brothers and sisters, who had discovered her weak point, amused themselves by scaring her. Lying in bed and hearing the tom-toms, she virtually *saw* Negroes. She fled under the covers, trembling. Then smaller and smaller circles appeared, blurring the Negroes. These circles are easily recognizable as a kind of defense mechanism against her hallucinosis. Later, the circles appeared without the Negroes—the defense mechanism had taken over without reference to what had brought it on.

I talked with the girl's mother, who corroborated what the patient had said. The girl was very emotional, and at the age of twelve she had often been observed to tremble in her bed. My presence on her ward made no perceptible difference in her mental state. By now it was the circles *alone* that produced the motor reactions: outcries, facial tics, random gesticulation.

Even when one concedes a constitutional factor here, it is clear that her alienation is the result of a fear of the Negro, a fear aggravated by determining circumstances. Although the patient had made considerable progress, it was doubtful whether she would soon be able to resume a normal life in society.

Chapter Seven

THE NEGRO AND RECOGNITION

A. *The Negro and Adler*

From whatever direction one approaches the analysis of abnormal psychogenic conditions, one very soon finds oneself in the presence of the following phenomenon: The whole picture of the neurosis, as well as all its symptoms, emerges as under the influence of some final goal, indeed as projections of this goal. Therefore one can ascribe the character of a formative cause to this final goal, the quality of a principle of orientation, of arrangement, of coordination. Try to understand the "meaning" and the direction of unhealthy manifestations, and you will immediately come face to face with a chaotic throng of tendencies, of impulses, of weaknesses and of anomalies, bound to discourage some and to arouse in others the rash resolve to penetrate the shadows at all costs, even at the risk of finding in the end that nothing has been gained, or that what has been gained is illusory. If, on the other hand, one accepts the hypothesis of a final goal or of a causal finality, one sees the shadows dissolve at once and we can read the soul of the patient like the pages of a book.[1]

It is on the basis of similar theoretical positions that,

1. Alfred Adler, *Le tempérament nerveux*, p. 12. (Originally, "Der nervöse charakter," in *Festschrift William Stern*, Leipzig, Barth, 1931).

in general, the most stupendous frauds of our period are constructed. Let us apply Adler's individual psychology to the Antilleans.

The Negro is comparison. There is the first truth. He is comparison: that is, he is constantly preoccupied with self-evaluation and with the ego-ideal. Whenever he comes into contact with someone else, the question of value, of merit, arises. The Antilleans have no inherent values of their own, they are always contingent on the presence of The Other. The question is always whether he is less intelligent than I, blacker than I, less respectable than I. Every position of one's own, every effort at security, is based on relations of dependence, with the diminution of the other. It is the wreckage of what surrounds me that provides the foundation for my virility.

I should like to suggest an experiment to any Martinican who reads this book: Find the most "comparative" street in Fort-de-France. Rue Schoelcher, rue Victor-Hugo—certainly not rue François-Arago. The Martinican who agrees to make this experiment will share my opinion precisely insofar as he can objectively endure seeing himself stripped naked. An Antillean who meets an acquaintance for the first time after five or six years' absence greets him with aggression. This is because in the past each had a fixed position. Now the inferior thinks that he has acquired worth . . . and the superior is determined to conserve the old hierarchy. "You haven't changed a bit . . . still as stupid as ever."

I have known some, physicians and dentists, who have gone on filling their heads with mistakes in judgment made fifteen years before. It is not so much conceptual errors as "Creolisms" with which the dangerous man is belabored. He was put in his place once and for all: nothing to be done about it. The Antillean is characterized by his desire to dominate the other. His line of orientation runs through the other. It is always a question of the subject; one never even thinks of the object. I try to read admiration in the eyes of the other, and if, unluckily, those eyes show me an unpleasant reflection, I find that mirror flawed: Unquestionably that other one is a fool. I do not try to be naked in the sight of the object. The object is denied in terms of individuality and liberty. The object is an instrument. It should enable me to realize my subjective security. I consider myself fulfilled (the wish for plenitude) and I recognize no division. The Other comes on to the stage only in order to furnish it. I am the Hero. Applaud or condemn, it makes no difference to me, I am the center of attention. If the other seeks to make me uneasy with his wish to have value (his fiction), I simply banish him without a trial. He ceases to exist. I don't want to hear about that fellow. I do not wish to experience the impact of the object. Contact with the object means conflict. I am Narcissus, and what I want to see in the eyes of others is a reflection that pleases me. Therefore, in any given group (environment) in Martinique, one finds the man on top, the court that surrounds him, the in-betweens (who are waiting for something better), and the losers. These last are slaughtered without mercy. One can imagine the temperature that prevails in that jungle. There is no way out of it.

Me, nothing but me.

The Martinicans are greedy for security. They want to compel the acceptance of their fiction. They want to be recognized in their quest for manhood. They want to make an appearance. Each one of them is an isolated, sterile, salient atom with sharply defined rights of passage, each one of them *is*. Each one of them wants to *be*, to *emerge*. Everything that an Antillean does is done for The Other.

Not because The Other is the ultimate objective of his action in the sense of communication between people that Adler describes,[2] but, more primitively, because it is The Other who corroborates him in his search for self-validation.

Now that we have marked out the Adlerian line of orientation of the Antillean, our task is to look for its source.

Here the difficulties begin. In effect, Adler has created a psychology of the individual. We have just seen that the feeling of inferiority is an Antillean characteristic. It is not just this or that Antillean who embodies the neurotic formation, but all Antilleans. Antillean society is a neurotic society, a society of "comparison." Hence we are driven from the individual back to the social structure. If there is a taint, it lies not in the "soul" of the individual but rather in that of the environment.

The Martinican is and is not a neurotic. If we were strict in applying the conclusions of the Adlerian school, we should say that the Negro is seeking to protest against the inferiority that he feels historically. Since in all periods the Negro has been an inferior, he attempts to react with a superiority complex. And this is indeed what comes out of Brachfeld's book. Discussing the feeling of racial inferiority, Brachfeld quotes a Spanish play by André de Claramunte, *El valiante negro de Flandres.* This play makes clear that the inferiority of the Negro does not date from this century, since De Claramunte was a contemporary of Lope de Vega:

> Only the color of his skin there lacked
> That he should be a man of gentle blood.

And the Negro, Juan de Mérida, says this:

2. In *Understanding Human Nature.*

What a disgrace it is to be black
in this world!
Are black men not
men?
Does that endow them with a baser soul,
a duller, an uglier?
And for that they have earned scornful
names.
I rise burdened with the shame of my
color
And I let the world know my courage . . .
Is it so vile to be black?

Poor Juan cannot be sure any longer what saint to invoke. Normally, the black man is a slave. There is nothing of that sort in his attitude:

For, though I be black,
I am not a slave.

Nevertheless he would like to be able to flee that blackness. He has an ethical position in the world. Viewed from an axiological standpoint, he is a white man:

I am more white than snow.

For, after all, on the symbolic level,

What is it really, then, to be black?
Is it being that color?
For that outrage I will denounce
fate,
my times, heaven,
and all those who made me black!
O curse of color!

In his isolation, Juan sees that the wish cannot save him. His *appearance* saps, invalidates, all his actions:

What do souls matter?
I am mad.

What can I do but despair?
O heaven what a dread thing
being black.

At the climax of his anguish there remains only one solution for the miserable Negro: furnish proofs of his whiteness to others and above all to himself.

If I cannot change my color
I want Luck.[3]

As we can see, Juan de Mérida must be understood from the viewpoint of overcompensation. It is because the Negro belongs to an "inferior" race that he seeks to be like the superior race.

But we have a means of shaking off the Adlerian leech. In the United States, De Man and Eastman have applied Adler's method somewhat excessively. All the facts that I have noted are real, but, it should not be necessary to point out, they have only a superficial connection with Adlerian psychology. The Martinican does not compare himself with the white man *qua* father, leader, God; he compares himself with his fellow against the pattern of the white man. An Adlerian comparison would be schematized in this fashion:

Ego greater than The Other

But the Antillean comparison, in contrast, would look like this:

$$\frac{\text{White}}{\text{Ego different from The Other}}$$

The Adlerian comparison embraces two terms; it is polarized by the ego. The Antillean comparison is surmounted by a third term: Its governing fiction is not personal but social.

3. My own translation from the Spanish—F.F.

The Martinican is a man crucified. The environment that has shaped him (but that he has not shaped) has horribly drawn and quartered him; and he feeds this cultural environment with his blood and his essences. Now, the blood of Negroes is a manure prized by experts.

If I were an Adlerian, then, having established the fact that my friend had fulfilled in a dream his wish to become white—that is, to be a man—I would show him that his neurosis, his psychic instability, the rupture of his ego arose out of this governing fiction, and I would say to him: "M. Mannoni has very ably described this phenomenon in the Malagasy. Look here: I think you simply have to resign yourself to remaining in the place that has been assigned to you."

Certainly not! I will not say that at all! I will tell him, "The environment, society are responsible for your delusion." Once that has been said, the rest will follow of itself, and what that is we know. The end of the world.

I wonder sometimes whether school inspectors and government functionaries are aware of the role they play in the colonies. For twenty years they poured every effort into programs that would make the Negro a white man. In the end, they dropped him and told him, "You have an indisputable complex of dependence on the white man."

B. The Negro and Hegel

> *Self-consciousness exists* in itself *and* for itself, *in that and by the fact that it exists for another self-consciousness; that is to say, it is only by being acknowledged or recognized.*
>
> —*Hegel,* The Phenomenology of Mind

Man is human only to the extent to which he tries to impose his existence on another man in order to be recognized by him. As long as he has not been effectively recognized by the other, that other will remain the theme of his actions. It is on that other being, on recognition by that other being, that his own human worth and reality depend. It is that other being in whom the meaning of his life is condensed.

There is not an open conflict between white and black. One day the White Master, *without conflict*, recognized the Negro slave.

But the former slave wants to *make himself recognized.*

At the foundation of Hegelian dialectic there is an absolute reciprocity which must be emphasized. It is in the degree to which I go beyond my own immediate being that I apprehend the existence of the other as a natural and more than natural reality. If I close the circuit, if I prevent the accomplishment of movement in two directions, I keep the other within himself. Ultimately, I deprive him even of this being-for-itself.

The only means of breaking this vicious circle that throws me back on myself is to restore to the other, through mediation and recognition, his human reality, which is different from natural reality. The other has to perform the same operation. "Action from one side only would be useless, because what is to happen can only be brought about by means of both. . . ."; "*they recognize themselves as mutually recognizing each other.*"[4]

In its immediacy, consciousness of self is simple being-for-itself. In order to win the certainty of oneself, the incorporation of the concept of recognition is essential. Similarly, the other is waiting for recognition by us, in order to burgeon into the universal consciousness of self. Each consciousness of self is in quest of absoluteness. It wants to be recognized as a primal value without reference

4. G. W. F. Hegel, *The Phenomenology of Mind*, trans. by J. B. Baillie, 2nd rev. ed. (London, Allen & Unwin, 1949), pp. 230, 231.

to life, as a transformation of subjective certainty (*Gewissheit*) into objective truth (*Wahrheit*).

When it encounters resistance from the other, self-consciousness undergoes the experience of *desire*—the first milestone on the road that leads to the dignity of the spirit. Self-consciousness accepts the risk of its life, and consequently it threatens the other in his physical being. "It is solely by risking life that freedom is obtained; only thus is it tried and proved that the essential nature of self-consciousness is not *bare existence*, is not the merely immediate form in which it at first makes its appearance, is not its mere absorption in the expanse of life."[5]

Thus human reality in-itself-for-itself can be achieved only through conflict and through the risk that conflict implies. This risk means that I go beyond life toward a supreme good that is the transformation of subjective certainty of my own worth into a universally valid objective truth.

As soon as I *desire* I am asking to be considered. I am not merely here-and-now, sealed into thingness. I am for somewhere else and for something else. I demand that notice be taken of my negating activity insofar as I pursue something other than life; insofar as I do battle for the creation of a human world—that is, of a world of reciprocal recognitions.

He who is reluctant to recognize me opposes me. In a savage struggle I am willing to accept convulsions of death, invincible dissolution, but also the possibility of the impossible.[6]

---

5. *Ibid.*, p. 233.

6. When I began this book, I wanted to devote one section to a study of the death wish among Negroes. I believed it necessary because people are forever saying that Negroes never commit suicide.

The other, however, can recognize me without struggle: "The individual, who has not staked his life, may, no doubt, be recognized as a *person*, but he has not attained the truth of this recognition as an independent self-consciousness."[7]

Historically, the Negro steeped in the inessentiality of servitude was set free by his master. He did not fight for his freedom.

Out of slavery the Negro burst into the lists where his masters stood. Like those servants who are allowed once every year to dance in the drawing room, the Negro is looking for a prop. The Negro has not become a master. When there are no longer slaves, there are no longer masters.

The Negro is a slave who has been allowed to assume the attitude of a master.

The white man is a master who has allowed his slaves to eat at his table.

M. Achille did not hesitate to maintain this in a lecture, and Richard Wright, in one of his stories, has a white character say, "If I were a Negro I'd kill myself . . . ," in the sense that only a Negro could submit to such treatment without feeling drawn to suicide.

Since then, M. Deshaies has taken the question of suicide as the subject of his thesis. He demonstrates that the studies by Jaensch, who contrasted the disintegrated-personality "type" (blue eyes, white skin) to the integrated-personality "type" (brown eyes and skin), are predominantly specious.

According to Durkheim, Jews never committed suicide. Now it is the Negroes. Very well: "The Detroit municipal hospital found that 16.6% of its suicide cases were Negroes, although the proportion of Negroes in the total population is only 7.6%. In Cincinnati, the number of Negro suicides is more than double that of whites; this may result in part from the amazing sexual disparity among Negro suicides: 358 women against 76 men." (Gabriel Deshaies, *Psychologie du suicide,* note 23.)

7. Hegel, *op. cit.,* p. 233.

One day a good white master who had influence said to his friends, "Let's be nice to the niggers. . . ."

The other masters argued, for after all it was not an easy thing, but then they decided to promote the machine-animal-men to the supreme rank of *men*.

Slavery shall no longer exist on French soil.

The upheaval reached the Negroes from without. The black man was acted upon. Values that had not been created by his actions, values that had not been born of the systolic tide of his blood, danced in a hued whirl round him. The upheaval did not make a difference in the Negro. He went from one way of life to another, but not from one life to another. Just as when one tells a much improved patient that in a few days he will be discharged from the hospital, he thereupon suffers a relapse, so the announcement of the liberation of the black slaves produced psychoses and sudden deaths.

It is not an announcement that one hears twice in a lifetime. The black man contented himself with thanking the white man, and the most forceful proof of the fact is the impressive number of statues erected all over France and the colonies to show white France stroking the kinky hair of this nice Negro whose chains had just been broken.

"Say thank you to the nice man," the mother tells her little boy . . . but we know that often the little boy is dying to scream some other, more resounding expression. . . .

The white man, in the capacity of master,[8] said to the Negro, "From now on you are free."

8. I hope I have shown that here the master differs basically from the master described by Hegel. For Hegel there is reciprocity; here the master laughs at the consciousness of the slave. What he wants from the slave is not recognition but work.

But the Negro knows nothing of the cost of freedom, for he has not fought for it. From time to time he has fought for Liberty and Justice, but these were always white liberty and white justice; that is, values secreted by his masters. The former slave, who can find in his memory no trace of the struggle for liberty or of that anguish of liberty of which Kierkegaard speaks, sits unmoved before the young white man singing and dancing on the tightrope of existence.

When it does happen that the Negro looks fiercely at the white man, the white man tells him: "Brother, there is no difference between us." And yet the Negro *knows* that there is a difference. He *wants* it. He wants the white man to turn on him and shout: "Damn nigger." Then he would have that unique chance—to "show them. . . ."

But most often there is nothing—nothing but indifference, or a paternalistic curiosity.

The former slave needs a challenge to his humanity, he wants a conflict, a riot. But it is too late: The French Negro is doomed to bite himself and just to bite. I say "the French Negro," for the American Negro is cast in a different play. In the United States, the Negro battles and is battled. There are laws that, little by little, are invalidated under the Constitution. There are other laws that forbid certain forms of discrimination. And we can be sure that nothing is going to be given free.

There is war, there are defeats, truces, victories.

In the same way, the slave here is in no way identifiable with the slave who loses himself in the object and finds in his work the source of his liberation.

The Negro wants to be like the master.

Therefore he is less independent than the Hegelian slave.

In Hegel the slave turns away from the master and turns toward the object.

Here the slave turns toward the master and abandons the object.

"The twelve million black voices"[9] howled against the curtain of the sky. Torn from end to end, marked with the gashes of teeth biting into the belly of interdiction, the curtain fell like a burst balloon.

On the field of battle, its four corners marked by the scores of Negroes hanged by their testicles, a monument is slowly being built that promises to be majestic.

And, at the top of this monument, I can already see a white man and a black man *hand in hand.*

For the French Negro the situation is unbearable. Unable ever to be sure whether the white man considers him consciousness in-itself-for-itself, he must forever absorb himself in uncovering resistance, opposition, challenge.

This is what emerges from some of the passages of the book that Mounier has devoted to Africa.[10] The young Negroes whom he knew there sought to maintain their alterity. Alterity of rupture, of conflict, of battle.

The self takes its place by opposing itself, Fichte said. Yes and no.

I said in my introduction that man is a *yes.* I will never stop reiterating that.

Yes to life. *Yes* to love. *Yes* to generosity.

But man is also a *no. No* to scorn of man. *No* to degradation of man. *No* to exploitation of man. *No* to the butchery of what is most human in man: freedom.

Man's behavior is not only reactional. And there is always resentment in a *reaction.* Nietzsche had already pointed that out in *The Will to Power.*

To educate man to be *actional,* preserving in all his relations his respect for the basic values that constitute a human world, is the prime task of him who, having taken thought, prepares to act.

---

9. In English in the original. (Translator's note.)

10. Emmanuel Mounier, *L'éveil de l'Afrique noire* (Paris, Éditions du Seuil, 1948).

Chapter Eight

BY WAY OF CONCLUSION

> *The social revolution . . . cannot draw its poetry from the past, but only from the future. It cannot begin with itself before it has stripped itself of all its superstitions concerning the past. Earlier revolutions relied on memories out of world history in order to drug themselves against their own content. In order to find their own content, the revolutions of the nineteenth century have to let the dead bury the dead. Before, the expression exceeded the content; now, the content exceeds the expression.*
>
> —*Karl Marx,* The Eighteenth Brumaire

I can already see the faces of all those who will ask me to be precise on this or that point, to denounce this or that mode of conduct.

It is obvious—and I will never weary of repeating this—that the quest for disalienation by a doctor of medicine born in Guadeloupe can be understood only by recognizing motivations basically different from those of the Negro laborer building the port facilities in Abidjan. In the first case, the alienation is of an almost intellectual character.

Insofar as he conceives of European culture as a means of stripping himself of his race, he becomes alienated. In the second case, it is a question of a victim of a system based on the exploitation of a given race by another, on the contempt in which a given branch of humanity is held by a form of civilization that pretends to superiority.

I do not carry innocence to the point of believing that appeals to reason or to respect for human dignity can alter reality. For the Negro who works on a sugar plantation in Le Robert, there is only one solution: to fight. He will embark on this struggle, and he will pursue it, not as the result of a Marxist or idealistic analysis but quite simply because he cannot conceive of life otherwise than in the form of a battle against exploitation, misery, and hunger.

It would never occur to me to ask these Negroes to change their conception of history. I am convinced, however, that without even knowing it they share my views, accustomed as they are to speaking and thinking in terms of the present. The few working-class people whom I had the chance to know in Paris never took it on themselves to pose the problem of the discovery of a Negro past. They knew they were black, but, they told me, that made no difference in anything. In which they were absolutely right.

In this connection, I should like to say something that I have found in many other writers: Intellectual alienation is a creation of middle-class society. What I call middle-class society is any society that becomes rigidified in predetermined forms, forbidding all evolution, all gains, all progress, all discovery. I call middle-class a closed society in which life has no taste, in which the air is tainted, in which ideas and men are corrupt. And I think that a man who takes a stand against this death is in a sense a revolutionary.

The discovery of the existence of a Negro civilization in the fifteenth century confers no patent of humanity on me. Like it or not, the past can in no way guide me in the present moment.

The situation that I have examined, it is clear by now, is not a classic one. Scientific objectivity was barred to me, for the alienated, the neurotic, was my brother, my sister, my father. I have ceaselessly striven to show the Negro that in a sense he makes himself abnormal; to show the white man that he is at once the perpetrator and the victim of a delusion.

There are times when the black man is locked into his body. Now, "for a being who has acquired consciousness of himself and of his body, who has attained to the dialectic of subject and object, the body is no longer a cause of the structure of consciousness, it has become an object of consciousness."[1]

The Negro, however sincere, is the slave of the past. None the less I am a man, and in this sense the Peloponnesian War is as much mine as the invention of the compass. Face to face with the white man, the Negro has a past to legitimate, a vengeance to exact; face to face with the Negro, the contemporary white man feels the need to recall the times of cannibalism. A few years ago, the Lyon branch of the Union of Students From Overseas France asked me to reply to an article that made jazz music literally an irruption of cannibalism into the modern world. Knowing exactly what I was doing, I

---

1. Maurice Merleau-Ponty, *La Phénoménologie de la perception* (Paris, Gallimard, 1945), p. 277.

rejected the premises on which the request was based, and I suggested to the defender of European purity that he cure himself of a spasm that had nothing cultural in it. Some men want to fill the world with their presence. A German philosopher described this mechanism as *the pathology of freedom.* In the circumstances, I did not have to take up a position on behalf of Negro music against white music, but rather to help my brother to rid himself of an attitude in which there was nothing healthful.

The problem considered here is one of time. Those Negroes and white men will be disalienated who refuse to let themselves be sealed away in the materialized Tower of the Past. For many other Negroes, in other ways, disalienation will come into being through their refusal to accept the present as definitive.

I am a man, and what I have to recapture is the whole past of the world. I am not responsible solely for the revolt in Santo Domingo.

Every time a man has contributed to the victory of the dignity of the spirit, every time a man has said no to an attempt to subjugate his fellows, I have felt solidarity with his act.

In no way should I derive my basic purpose from the past of the peoples of color.

In no way should I dedicate myself to the revival of an unjustly unrecognized Negro civilization. I will not make myself the man of any past. I do not want to exalt the past at the expense of my present and of my future.

It is not because the Indo-Chinese has discovered a culture of his own that he is in revolt. It is because "quite simply" it was, in more than one way, becoming impossible for him to breathe. When one remembers the stories with which, in 1938, old regular sergeants described the land of piastres and rickshaws, of cut-rate boys and women, one understands only too well the rage with which the men of the Viet-Minh go into battle.

An acquaintance with whom I served during the Second World War recently returned from Indo-China. He has enlightened me on many things. For instance, the serenity with which young Vietnamese of sixteen or seventeen faced firing squads. "On one occasion," he told me, "we had to shoot from a kneeling position: The soldiers' hands were shaking in the presence of those young 'fanatics.'" Summing up, he added: "The war that you and I were in was only a game compared to what is going on out there."

Seen from Europe, these things are beyond understanding. There are those who talk of a so-called Asiatic attitude toward death. But these basement philosophers cannot convince anyone. This Asiatic serenity, not so long ago, was a quality to be seen in the "bandits" of Vercors and the "terrorists" of the Resistance.

The Vietnamese who die before the firing squads are not hoping that their sacrifice will bring about the reappearance of a past. It is for the sake of the present and of the future that they are willing to die.

If the question of practical solidarity with a given past ever arose for me, it did so only to the extent to which I was committed to myself and to my neighbor to fight for all my life and with all my strength so that never again would a people on the earth be subjugated. It was not the black world that laid down my course of conduct. My black skin is not the wrapping of specific values. It is a long time since the starry sky that took away Kant's breath revealed the last of its secrets to us. And the moral law is not certain of itself.

As a man, I undertake to face the possibility of annihilation in order that two or three truths may cast their eternal brilliance over the world.

Sartre has shown that, in the line of an unauthentic position, the past "takes" in quantity, and, when solidly constructed, *informs* the individual. He is the past in a changed value. But, too, I can recapture my past, validate it, or condemn it through my successive choices.

The black man wants to be like the white man. For the black man there is only one destiny. And it is white. Long ago the black man admitted the unarguable superiority of the white man, and all his efforts are aimed at achieving a white existence.

Have I no other purpose on earth, then, but to avenge the Negro of the seventeenth century?

In this world, which is already trying to disappear, do I have to pose the problem of black truth?

Do I have to be limited to the justification of a facial conformation?

I as a man of color do not have the right to seek to know in what respect my race is superior or inferior to another race.

I as a man of color do not have the right to hope that in the white man there will be a crystallization of guilt toward the past of my race.

I as a man of color do not have the right to seek ways of stamping down the pride of my former master.

I have neither the right nor the duty to claim reparation for the domestication of my ancestors.

There is no Negro mission; there is no white burden.

I find myself suddenly in a world in which things do evil; a world in which I am summoned into battle; a world in which it is always a question of annihilation or triumph.

I find myself—I, a man—in a world where words wrap themselves in silence; in a world where the other endlessly hardens himself.

No, I do not have the right to go and cry out my hatred at the white man. I do not have the duty to murmur my gratitude to the white man.

My life is caught in the lasso of existence. My freedom turns me back on myself. No, I do not have the right to be a Negro.

I do not have the duty to be this or that. . . .

If the white man challenges my humanity, I will impose my whole weight as a man on his life and show him that I am not that "sho' good eatin'" that he persists in imagining.

I find myself suddenly in the world and I recognize that I have one right alone: That of demanding human behavior from the other.

One duty alone: That of not renouncing my freedom through my choices.

I have no wish to be the victim of the *Fraud* of a black world.

My life should not be devoted to drawing up the balance sheet of Negro values.

There is no white world, there is no white ethic, any more than there is a white intelligence.

There are in every part of the world men who search.

I am not a prisoner of history. I should not seek there for the meaning of my destiny.

I should constantly remind myself that the real *leap* consists in introducing invention into existence.

In the world through which I travel, I am endlessly creating myself.

I am a part of Being to the degree that I go beyond it.

And, through a private problem, we see the outline of

the problem of Action. Placed in this world, in a situation, "embarked," as Pascal would have it, am I going to gather weapons?

Am I going to ask the contemporary white man to answer for the slave-ships of the seventeenth century?

Am I going to try by every possible means to cause Guilt to be born in minds?

Moral anguish in the face of the massiveness of the Past? I am a Negro, and tons of chains, storms of blows, rivers of expectoration flow down my shoulders.

But I do not have the right to allow myself to bog down. I do not have the right to allow the slightest fragment to remain in my existence. I do not have the right to allow myself to be mired in what the past has determined.

I am not the slave of the Slavery that dehumanized my ancestors.

To many colored intellectuals European culture has a quality of exteriority. What is more, in human relationships, the Negro may feel himself a stranger to the Western world. Not wanting to live the part of a poor relative, of an adopted son, of a bastard child, shall he feverishly seek to discover a Negro civilization?

Let us be clearly understood. I am convinced that it would be of the greatest interest to be able to have contact with a Negro literature or architecture of the third century before Christ. I should be very happy to know that a correspondence had flourished between some Negro philosopher and Plato. But I can absolutely not see how this fact would change anything in the lives of the eight-year-old children who labor in the cane fields of Martinique or Guadeloupe.

No attempt must be made to encase man, for it is his destiny to be set free.

The body of history does not determine a single one of my actions.

I am my own foundation.

And it is by going beyond the historical, instrumental hypothesis that I will initiate the cycle of my freedom.

The disaster of the man of color lies in the fact that he was enslaved.

The disaster and the inhumanity of the white man lie in the fact that somewhere he has killed man.

And even today they subsist, to organize this dehumanization rationally. But I as a man of color, to the extent that it becomes possible for me to exist absolutely, do not have the right to lock myself into a world of retroactive reparations.

I, the man of color, want only this:

That the tool never possess the man. That the enslavement of man by man cease forever. That is, of one by another. That it be possible for me to discover and to love man, wherever he may be.

The Negro is not. Any more than the white man.

Both must turn their backs on the inhuman voices which were those of their respective ancestors in order that authentic communication be possible. Before it can adopt a positive voice, freedom requires an effort at disalienation. At the beginning of his life a man is always clotted, he is drowned in contingency. The tragedy of the man is that he was once a child.

It is through the effort to recapture the self and to scrutinize the self, it is through the lasting tension of their freedom that men will be able to create the ideal conditions of existence for a human world.

Superiority? Inferiority?

Why not the quite simple attempt to touch the other, to feel the other, to explain the other to myself?

Was my freedom not given to me then in order to build the world of the *You*?

At the conclusion of this study, I want the world to recognize, with me, the open door of every consciousness.

My final prayer:

O my body, make of me always a man who questions!